INTRODUCTION TO PHILOSOPHY: PHILOSOPHY OF MIND

ERAN ASOULIN, PAUL RICHARD BLUM, TONY CHENG, DANIEL HAAS, JASON NEWMAN, HENRY SHEVLIN, ELLY VINTIADIS, HEATHER SALAZAR (EDITOR), AND CHRISTINA HENDRICKS (SERIES EDITOR)

Rebus Community

CONTENTS

WHAT IS AN OPEN TEXTBOOK?

CHRISTINA HENDRICKS

An open textbook is like a commercial textbook, except: (1) it is publicly available online free of charge (and at low-cost in print), and (2) it has an open license that allows others to reuse it, download and revise it, and redistribute it. This book has a Creative Commons Attribution license, which allows reuse, revision, and redistribution so long as the original creator is attributed (please see the licensing information for this book for more information).

In addition to saving students money, an open textbook can be revised to be better contextualized to one's own teaching. In a recent study of undergraduate students in an introductory level physics course, students reported that the thing they most appreciated about the open textbook used in that course was that it was customized to fit the course, followed very closely by the fact that it was free of cost (Hendricks, Reinsberg, and Rieger 2017). For example, in an open textbook one may add in examples more relevant to one's own context or the topic of a course, or embedded slides, videos, or other resources. Note from the licensing information for this book that one must clarify in such cases that the book is an adaptation.

A number of commercial publishers offer relatively inexpensive digital textbooks (whether on their own or available through an access code that students must pay to purchase), but these may have certain limitations and other issues:

- Access for students is often limited to a short period of time;
- Students cannot buy used copies from others, nor sell their own copies to others, to save money;
- Depending on the platform, there may be limits to how students can interact with and take notes on the books (and they may not be able to export their notes outside the book, so lose access to those as well when they lose access to the book).

None of these is the case with open textbooks like the Introduction to Philosophy series. Students can download any book in this series and keep it for as long as they wish. They can interact with it in multiple formats: on the web; as editable word processing formats; offline as PDF, EPUB; as a physical print book, and more.

See the next section, "How to Access and Use the Books," for more information on what the open license on this book allows, and how to properly attribute the work when reusing, redistributing, or adapting.

HOW TO ACCESS AND USE THE BOOKS

CHRISTINA HENDRICKS

We hope the books (or chapters in the books) will be adopted for introductory-level courses in philosophy, as part of required readings. You may use the books as they are, or create adaptations or ancillaries. One of the important benefits of the Introduction to Philosophy series is that instructors can mix and match chapters from various books to make their own customized set of readings for their courses.

Be sure to read the licensing information carefully and attribute the chapters or book properly when reusing, redistributing, or adapting.

Each book can be read online, and is also downloadable in multiple formats, from their respective book home pages on the Rebus Press site (e.g., Introduction to the Philosophy of Mind).

- The .odt format can be opened by Open Office, Libre Office, or Microsoft Word. Note that there may be some issues with formatting on this format, and hyperlinks may not appear if opened with MS Word.

- The PDF files can be edited with Adobe Acrobat (the full program, not just the Reader) or printed out. The print version of the PDF does not have hyperlinks.

- The EPUB and MOBI files can be loaded onto digital reading platforms like Adobe Digital Editions, Apple Books, and Kindle. They can also be edited using Pressbooks or tools like Calibre.

- Edits can be made using the XHTML format or via the Pressbooks XML format (for easier adaptation in Pressbooks).

- The book is also available for download as a Common Cartridge 1.1 file (with web links) for import into your learning management system (see instructions for importing Common Cartridge files, from the Pressbooks User Guide).

The multiple editable formats allow instructors to adapt the books as needed to fit their contexts. Another way to create adaptations is to involve students in contributing to open textbooks. Students may add new sections to an adapted book, link to other resources, create discussion questions or quiz questions, and more. Please see Rebus Community's *A Guide to Making Open Textbooks with Students* for more information and ideas.

If you plan to use or adapt one or more books (or chapters), we'd love to hear about it! Please let us know on the Rebus Community platform, and also on our adoption form.

And if you have feedback or suggestions about the book, we would really appreciate those as well. We have a separate form for keeping track of issues with digital accessibility, so please let us know if you find any.

INTRODUCTION TO THE SERIES

CHRISTINA HENDRICKS

This book is part of the *Introduction to Philosophy* open textbook series, a set of nine (and counting?) open access textbooks that are designed to be used for introductory-level, survey courses in philosophy at the post-secondary level.

OVERVIEW OF THE SERIES

This set of books is meant to provide an introduction to some of the major topic areas often covered in introductory-level philosophy courses. I have found in teaching students new to philosophy that many struggle with the new ideas, questions, and approaches they find in introductory courses in philosophy, and that it can be helpful to provide them with texts that explain these in relatively straightforward terms.

When I began this project there were few textbooks that I was happy enough with to ask students to purchase, and even fewer openly licensed textbooks that I could pick and choose chapters from, or revise, to suit my courses. This series was created out of a desire to provide such resources that can be customized to fit different contexts and updated by instructors when needed (rather than waiting for an updated version from a publisher).

Each book is designed to be accessible to students who have little to no background in philosophy, by either eliminating jargon or providing a glossary for specialized philosophical terms. Many chapters in the books provide examples that apply philosophical questions or concepts to concrete objects or experiences that, we hope, many students are familiar with. Questions for reflection and discussion accompany chapters in most of the books, to support students in understanding what to focus on as they are reading.

The chapters in the books provide a broad overview of some of the main discussions and debates in the philosophical literature within a topic area, from the perspective of the chapter authors. Some of the chapters focus on historical approaches and debates, such as ancient theories of aesthetics, substance dualism in Descartes, or classical utilitarian versus Kantian approaches in ethics. Others introduce students to questions and topics in the philosophical literature from just the last few decades.

The books currently in production for the series are:

- *Aesthetics* (Ed. Valery Vinogradovs and Scott Clifton): chapters include ancient aesthetics; beauty in art and nature; the nature of art, art and emotions, art and morality, recent aesthetics

- *Epistemology* (Ed. Brian Barnett): chapters include epistemic justification; rationalism, empiricism and beyond; skepticism; epistemic value, duty, and virtue; epistemology, gender, and society

- *Ethics* (Ed. George Matthews): chapters include ethical relativism, divine command theory and natural law; ethical egoism and social contract theory; virtue ethics; utilitarianism; Kantianism; feminist ethics

- *Metaphysics* (Ed. Adriano Palma): chapters include universals; finitism, infinitism, monism, dualism, pluralism; the possibility of free action; experimental metaphysics

- *Philosophy of Mind* (Ed. Heather Salazar): chapters include Descartes and substance dualism; behaviourism and materialism; functionalism; qualia; freedom of the will

- *Philosophy of Religion* (Ed. Beau Branson): chapters include arguments for belief in God; reasons not to believe; arguments against belief from the cognitive science of religion; critical perspectives on the philosophy of religion as a philosophy of theism

- *Philosophy of Science* (Ed. Eran Asoulin): chapters include empiricism, Popper's conjectures and refutations; Kuhn's normal and revolutionary science; the sociology of scientific knowledge; feminism and the philosophy of science; the problem of induction; explanation

- *Social and Political Philosophy* (Ed. TBA and Douglas Giles): chapters include the ideal society; the state of nature and the modern state; human rights, liberty, and social justice; radical social theories

We envision the books as helping to orient students within the topic areas covered by the chapters, as well as to introduce them to influential philosophical questions and approaches in an accessible way. The books may be used for course readings on their own, or in conjunction with primary source texts by the philosophers discussed in the chapters. We aim thereby to both save students money and to provide a relatively easy route for instructors to customize and update the resources as needed. And we hope that future adaptations will be shared back with the rest of the philosophical community!

HOW THE BOOKS WERE PRODUCED

Contributors to this series have been crowdsourced through email lists, social media, and other means. Each of the books has its own editor, and multiple authors from different parts of the world who have expertise in the topic of the book. This also means that there will inevitably be shifts in voice and tone between chapters, as well as in perspectives. This itself exemplifies the practice of philosophy, insofar as the philosophical questions worth discussing are those that do not yet have settled answers, and towards which there are multiple approaches worthy of consideration (which must, of course, provide arguments to support their claim to such worth).

I have been thrilled with the significant interest these books have generated, such that so many people have been willing to volunteer their time to contribute to them and ensure their quality—not only through careful writing and editing, but also through extensive feedback and review. Each book in the series has between five and ten authors, plus an editor and peer reviewers. It's exciting to see so many philosophers willing to contribute to a project devoted to helping students save money and instructors customize their textbooks!

The book editors, each with expertise in the field of the book they have edited, have done the bulk of the work for the books. They created outlines of chapters that were then peer reviewed and revised accordingly, and they selected authors for each of the chapters. The book editors worked with authors to develop a general approach to each chapter, and coordinated timelines for their completion. Chapters were reviewed by the editors both before and after the books went out for peer review, and the editors ensured revisions occurred where needed. They have also written introductions to their books, and in some cases other chapters as well. As the subject experts for the books, they have had the greatest influence on the content of each book.

My role as series editor started by envisioning the project as a whole and discussing what it might look like with a significant number of philosophers who contributed to shaping it early on. Overall, I have worked the Rebus Community on project management, such as developing author and reviewer guidelines and other workflows, coordinating with the book editors to ensure common approaches across the books, sending out calls for contributors to recruit new participants, and updating the community on the status of the project through the Rebus Community platform. I have reviewed the books, along with peer reviewers, from the perspective of both a philosopher who teaches introductory-level courses and a reader who is not an expert in many of the fields the books cover. As the books near publication, I have coordinated copy editing and importing into the Pressbooks publishing platform (troubleshooting where needed along the way).

Finally, after publication of the books I and the book editors will be working on spreading the word about them and encouraging adoption. I plan to use chapters from a few of the books in my own Introduction to Philosophy courses, and hope to see many more adoptions to come.

This project has been multiple years in the making, and we hope the fruits of our many labours are taken up in philosophy courses!

PRAISE FOR THE BOOK

ADRIANO PALMA

In a breezy introduction to the philosophy of mind edited by Heather Salazar, the beginner reader is immersed in an easy way into issues that are not otherwise easy to grasp, such as why one must interpret differently 'taking the child back to the zoo' and 'taking the car back to the zoo', and what makes it very hard to tell a vegetarian what octopus salad tastes like.

All the same the reader gets the right glimpse of why, centuries after they were written, the ideas of Descartes and Hobbes are relevant to the presence of zombies among us, or the scary prospect that the arguments to the effect that we are the zombies are correct.

An excellent way to start a class on the philosophy of mind, without being bogged down from the get go into the synapses that got away.

— Adriano Palma, University of KwaZulu-Natal, Durban, South Africa

ACKNOWLEDGEMENTS

HEATHER SALAZAR AND CHRISTINA HENDRICKS

HEATHER SALAZAR, BOOK EDITOR

Everyone who worked on this book generously donated their time and expertise to ensure that students in philosophy of mind have an engaging and well-researched contemporary introduction that is freely accessible.

This book is a part of a series that was envisioned by Christina Hendricks. Her foresight, flexibility, and cooperation were essential in bringing this book to fruition. Apurva Ashok, our project manager for the series at the Rebus Foundation, was indispensable. She kindly supported us in our vision and promptly answered all of my questions. I could not have asked for a more responsive publisher. I was pleased that my own artwork was chosen for the cover and Jonathan Lashley, who designed the cover, made it look striking and modern. Our book was peer-reviewed by Adriano Palma, who made astute observations and enabled us to edit the chapters quickly and confidently.

Finally, many thanks to the contributors to this volume. Our chapters are written by excellent scholars who worked through revisions as responsibly as they would have had they contributed to a standard textbook. The result is an introduction to philosophy of mind that instructors can confidently use in their classes.

CHRISTINA HENDRICKS, SERIES EDITOR

I would like to thank the authors in this book for their patience as we worked through the process of conceiving the book and getting it to publication. Because this is the first book to be published in the Introduction to Philosophy open textbook series, we were sometimes creating processes and workflows as we went along, and this meant things may have taken longer than anyone expected at first!

I would also like to thank Adriano Palma for his careful peer review of the chapters in this book. (And sneak preview, he is also an editor for another book in the series, Introduction to Metaphysics!)

Special thanks to Heather Salazar for her excellent and attentive work in editing this book. She has been eminently flexible as we worked through the kinks of getting the first book in the series published, and unfailingly patient as I faced the realization of just how many time-consuming steps were needed for that to happen. I am also thrilled that she agreed to provide one of her original artworks for the cover, which fits the book perfectly.

Speaking of the cover, I met Jonathan Lashley when we were both OER Research Fellows with the Open Education Group, and I didn't realize he had design talent until he saw one of my messages on social media and volunteered to help. I was floored by the designs he created for the book series, and it was very difficult to choose just one among the beautiful options he drafted. The book covers are exceptionally well done, and really bring the series together as a whole.

In the last weeks before publication, Colleen Cressman stepped in to provide much-needed help with copyediting. I am very grateful for her thorough and detailed efforts, and for the suggestions she made to help make the chapters as accessible as possible for introductory-level students. At the same time, Nate Angell contributed his expertise with the Pressbooks platform and did a wonderful job inputting many, many google documents into Pressbooks and formatting the content so that it looks and reads well. I particularly appreciated his help with importing LaTeX code into Pressbooks for one of the chapters, which is something it would have taken me a long time to figure out how to do!

When I started this project there were many discussions amongst philosophers from various parts of the world on the Rebus Community platform, and their ideas and suggestions contributed significantly to the final products. There were also numerous people who gave comments on draft chapter outlines for each book. Thank you to the many unnamed philosophers who have contributed to the book in these and other ways!

This book series would not have gotten beyond the idea stage were it not for the support of the Rebus Community. I want to thank Hugh McGuire for believing in the project enough to support what we both realized at the time was probably much bigger than even our apprehensions about its enormity. Zoe Wake Hyde was instrumental in getting the project started, particularly in helping us develop workflows and documentation. And I'm not sure I can ever thank Apurva Ashok enough for being an unfailingly enthusiastic and patient supporter and guide for more months than I care to count. She spent a good deal of time working with me and the book editors to figure out how to make a project like this work on a day-to-day level, and taught me a great deal about the open publishing process. Apurva kept me on track when I would sometimes drop the ball or get behind on this off-the-side-of-my-desk project. She is one of the best collaborative partners I have never (yet!) met in person.

Finally, I want to thank my family for understanding how important this work is and why I have chosen to stay up late so many nights to do it. And for their patience on the many groggy, pre-coffee mornings that followed.

INTRODUCTION TO THE BOOK

HEATHER SALAZAR

The main questions in the philosophy of mind are derived from puzzles involving trying to develop a coherent theory of the nature and functions of the mind. Beginning with the nature of the mind, they include: Are minds separate from bodies or is the mind really just the body? If the mind is immaterial and the body material, how do they interact? How can this fit in with science? If the mind is just the body, then how is consciousness explained? How can we have experiences or free will to think and act? How can we explain the special relationship we seem to have with knowing our own mental states?

There are two major views in the philosophy of mind that arise from trying to describe the nature of our minds. One claims that our minds are different in nature and separate from our bodies and the other claims that our minds really are just physical, or a part of our bodies and the rest of the purely physical world. These mark the two extremes. The first is called "substance dualism" or "Cartesian dualism" after René Descartes, who originated the primary arguments and the general view. The other is called "physicalism" and was in the modern era associated most with Thomas Hobbes. Both philosophers were trying to make sense of the mind within the modern context of science within the latter part of the seventeenth century. Philosophy of mind was not yet a separate discipline and fell under metaphysics as these philosophers studied it, but this time period, called the modern period, marks the beginning of what we consider now to be investigations into the philosophy of mind. It was a period of great scientific advancement and marked the beginning of the discipline of psychology, as well.

Whereas substance or Cartesian dualism has a difficult time making sense in a scientific context, eliminative or reductive physicalism—which completely reduces or eliminates the mind to matter—has a difficult time making sense of the functions of our mind. Substance or Cartesian dualism (Chapter 1) and reductive or eliminative physicalism (Chapter 2) are two extremes in the philosophy of mind. These two theories have been largely replaced by views that are more compromising in nature within the past century when philosophy of mind as a discipline of its own dramatically burgeoned. The different theories can be arranged roughly on a continuum, starting with the most reductive to the least reductive theory: eliminative physicalism, eliminative behaviorism, type identity theory (Chapter 2), functionalism (Chapter 3), token identity theory (also often under the name property dualism; Chapter 4) and substance dualism (Chapter 1).

The more inner the mental phenomenon is, the more difficulty the physicalist theories will have making sense of it. For this reason, the philosophy of mind must attempt to make sense of inner states that appear subjective, whether of a feeling or of a thinking nature (Chapter 5). Theories about the status of such inner states and how our minds interact with the world involve discussions about diverse topics such as the nature of consciousness (Chapter 6), mental concepts (Chapter 7), and freedom of the will (Chapter 8).

CHAPTER 1.

SUBSTANCE DUALISM IN DESCARTES

PAUL RICHARD BLUM

INTRODUCTION

René Descartes (1596-1650) was a French philosopher who is often studied as the first great philosopher in the era of "modern philosophy." He is the most famous proponent of a view called "substance dualism," which states that the mind and the body are two different substances. While the body is material (corporeal), the mind is immaterial (incorporeal). This view leaves room for human souls, which are usually understood as immaterial. Descartes argued on the basis of the Christian views that souls are immaterial and can exist separate from the body, but he emphasized that the mind alone is immaterial, whereas the other traditional functions of the souls can be explained as corporeal operations. His view and arguments were so influential that after him many philosophers referred to substance dualism under Descartes' name as "Cartesian dualism." In his explanation of the mind, the soul, and the ability of humans to understand the world around them through the powers of their minds, Descartes remains one of the most influential figures not just in modern philosophy, but throughout the history of philosophy. Even in the contemporary era, philosophers such as Gilbert Ryle (1900-1976) found worth in writing about and arguing against Descartes' views to set up their own theories. Ryle questioned whether the mind and body are in fact distinct and argued that they would not communicate with each other if they were. Ryle states:

> Body and mind are ordinarily harnessed together….[T]he things and events which belong to the physical world…are external, while the workings of [a person's] own mind are internal….[This results in the] partly metaphorical representation of the bifurcation of a person's two lives. (1945, 11-16)

Ryle stated that, if Descartes' theory were correct, the mind would be a mere "ghost in a machine," inactive and unable to cause actions in the body (the machine). Ryle did not term Descartes' theory "substance dualism" but "Descartes' myth." Descartes' arguments for substance dualism and the immaterial nature of the mind and soul are therefore paramount to any investigation of the philosophy of mind, and are still being debated in present-day theories. On the other hand, with his interpretation of what he calls passions (most operations of a living body), he also provides incentives for a non-dualistic physicalism of the mind.

THE TRADITIONAL CONCEPT OF SUBSTANCE

Descartes' philosophy of mind was a response to the erosion of the traditional Aristotelian concept of substance after the Middle Ages. According to the Aristotelian view, any substance is composed of matter that is determined by the form that is its essence. So every living thing is a body conjoined with its soul (namely, what makes it alive as such or such thing). In other words, an animal is an animate body. The soul of a dog makes that bundle of flesh and bones a dog. The peculiar case of human beings is that this soul is also an intellect: the rational mind. In that case then, the soul (and certainly the mind) is something other than body; it is non-material (or incorporeal) because it forms and enlivens the material body. So the question arises: is the soul (or at least the human mind) something that exists on its own?

In the traditional Aristotelian approach, the form of a ship (what makes it look like a ship and makes the ship body float on water) is nothing separate from the ship, except that we can have a concept of it even if there is no ship around. But what about the form of a plant or an animal? The form of plants and animals is their soul. When they are destroyed, their form that makes them alive (with growth, movement, and senses) is gone. With human beings, that might be different: the mind may survive the death of the body. Some ancient thinkers argued that the mind or the soul survives death and enters another body, be that a person or a beast: the transmigration of souls or reincarnation. The Christian theory of humans teaches that the soul of an individual is created at the same time as the person; however, it lives on after the death of the person: the human intellect is immaterial and immortal. This is why some Christians venerate saints, and why some occultists invoke deceased persons for conversation.

 The essence of things (whether an artifact like a ship or the souls of plants, animals, and humans) was termed the thing's "substantial form." Forms make and express the substance of things. The thing's substantial form makes a thing what it is, and makes it possible to conceive of it and to know it.

This is where Descartes starts his theory of substances. In a letter to Henricus Regius (1598-1679), Descartes states that he does not reject substantial forms but finds them "unnecessary in setting out my explanations" (AT III492, CSM III 205).[1] He clearly sees them as a mere explanatory tool that may be replaced by a better one. Instead, Descartes suggests any material thing is only an aggregate of qualities and properties. He argues, in the same letter, against the habit to apply "substantial form" when defining the human being. He warns that to speak of substantial form both for humans and material things carries the risk to misunderstand the soul as something corporeal and material. Instead, he suggests limiting the term "substantial form" to the immaterial human soul alone in order to emphasize that the soul's nature is "quite different" from the essence of things that "emerge from the potentiality of matter." He says that "[T]his difference in nature opens the easiest route to demonstrating [the soul's] non-materiality and immortality" (AT III 503, 505; CSM III 208). In order to elevate the soul to a level above bodily things, he downplays non-human things to mere upshots of matter. This letter shows that Descartes' primary concerns are with method more than with facts and that he aims at separating material fields of knowledge from the soul.

---

1. Descartes' works are cited by the standard French edition C. Adam and P. Tannery (eds.), *Oeuvres de Descartes*. Paris: Vrin, 1964-1976, "AT" with volume and page number; the standard English translation J. G. Cottingham, R. Stoothoff, D. Murdoch, and A. Kenny (trs.), *The Philosophical Writings of Descartes*, 3 vols. Cambridge: Cambridge University Press, 1985-1991, "CSM" with volume and page number.

THE IMMATERIAL NATURE OF THE SOUL

Descartes attempts to reconcile having an immaterial soul within a largely scientific (and physicalist) framework. This leads to some surprising turns within his theory that are quite different from previous theories on substances. Ultimately, Descartes' view is dualist because, although he renders all earthly substances material (and understandable to science), one thing remains that is a true immaterial substance with an essence: the human soul. Animals and human bodies, because they are parts of the physical world, are not strictly substances with essences; they are more properly aggregates. He argues from what we can know (epistemology) instead of what there is (metaphysics), and this method directs his views on substances.

From the very beginning of his research, Descartes aimed at exploring the competence of thought in ascertaining knowledge, and in doing so he wrote *Rules for the Direction of the Mind* in search for assurance in science. This view would later be called "rationalism" because he prioritized the functions of intellect, imagination, sense perception, and memory. Rationalism influenced a long line of philosophers from the modern era throughout the contemporary era in philosophy. He later recommended a reduction of human knowledge from simple concepts and propositions. This method, as expounded in Rule XII, relies on the human mind as a "power." He states:

> As for the objects of knowledge, it is enough if we examine the following three questions: What presents itself to us spontaneously? How can one thing be known on the basis of something else? What conclusions can be drawn from each of these?

Notice his emphasis on the understanding of objective knowledge. The question is not "What *is* it?" but "How does it *appear* to me?" and "How does it connect with what I know?" Investigating the nature of the mind is of primary importance. Knowledge of objects themselves takes a back seat to the inner workings of the mind.

Descartes describes the intellect as "the power through which we know things in the strict sense [that] is purely spiritual, and is … distinct from the whole body." To explain this power is difficult; Descartes explains that "nothing quite like this power is to be found in corporeal things." It is the intellect that applies itself to seeing, touching, and so on; and only it can "act on its own," that is, to understand. Although it may appear to be a trifle, Descartes does not make positive claims here, but buffers everything with "it is said" (*dicitur*): the mind "is said" to see, touch, imagine, or understand. What counts is that this mental power can both receive sense data and refer to themes that have nothing corporeal at all (AT X 410-417, CSM I 39-43).

In his last work, *The Passions of the Soul*, Descartes focuses on those activities that are not thoughts in the abstract sense but "passions": "those perceptions, sensations or emotions of the soul which we refer particularly to it" (AT XI 349, CSM I 338f., art. 27). The body has a number of functions (movement, for instance); and the soul has two basic functions that are kinds of thought, namely, volition and perceptions. Volitions are activities, whereas perceptions are passive motions that do not originate from the soul itself (AT XI 349, CSM I 338f., art. 17). If a person desires something or resolves to do something, that is an activity of the soul; if a person sees or hears something, that impression does not come from inside but from outside—the soul is affected rather than active. This soul is not a member of the body; therefore, it has the surprising property not to have any location in the body, but to be "really joined to the whole body" precisely for being non-local, not extended, and immaterial. On the one hand, Descartes is reiterating the traditional Aristotelian understanding of ensoulment (the soul as shorthand for the life of animated things); on the other hand, he is enforcing the concept of body as a whole organism: since the soul is conjoined with the body as a whole, body and soul together appear to be an organism. The organism is an ensemble ("assemblage") of material function (AT XI 351, CSM I 339, art. 30). A strictly physicalist and non-dualist explanation of sensations and passions is lurking in the background. Under a physicalist (i.e. materialist) view, everything (including the mind) can be explained physically; there is no need to refer to anything outside physics. The stakes are high for a philosophy of mind because conceiving of the body as an organism might lead to explaining all psychical movements as mere functioning of body parts. Descartes moves boldly in this direction.

The questions he answers in this treatise, *The Passions of the Soul*, before classifying and explaining the six basic passions, are: How are these corporeal passions conveyed to the mind and how does the mind impact bodily functions due to emotions? To answer these questions, Descartes employs the Stoic concept of animal spirits. According to the Stoic theory, a tenuous body, located in the brain, links the mind with corporeal operations. This view was *en vogue* in the early seventeenth century, for instance in Tommaso Campanella (1568-1639) (1999). Descartes' animal spirits are "a certain very fine air or wind" that shuttle between the brain and the body parts (AT XI 332, CSM I 330, art. 7; Sepper 2016, 26-28). They must be like little messengers that travel between body parts and mind and seem to understand both languages of the body and mind. They are called "spirits" but are expressly described as very fine bodies coming from the blood. In order to make that plausible, an example Descartes gives will help.

> Wonder is a sudden surprise of the soul….It has two causes: first, an impression in the brain, which represents the object as something unusual and consequently worthy of special consideration; and secondly, a movement of the spirits, which the impression disposes both to flow with great force to the place in the brain where it is located so as to strengthen and preserve it there, and also to pass into the muscles which serve to keep the sense organs fixed in the same orientation so that they will continue to maintain the impression in the way in which they formed it. (AT XI 380f., CSM I 353, art. 70)

But how do those minute spirits work to communicate with the mind? Descartes points to the pineal gland, which was the only part in the brain that he knew of that did not come in pairs. This gland, however, is not where Descartes claims the soul resides; the soul itself has no location at all and is tied to the body as a whole. Rather, the fine spirits that fill the cavities of the brain use the gland to unite images and other sense impressions; and it is here where the mind "exercises its functions more particularly than in the other parts of the body" (AT XI 353f., CSM I 339f., art. 30f). The animal spirits mediate between body and mind.

We are left with an apparently strictly physicalist explanation of a great deal of mental activity in a strongly dualist conception of mind.[2] For the soul is a substance and it is of a totally different nature than body. Moreover, the traditionally so termed "lower faculties" of the soul (growth, movement, and sensations), which are equally present in animals, are removed from the definition of the human soul and ascribed to the body as an organism. Thinking (beyond the corporeal) is now the only the activity of the soul. Traditionally, thinking had been the privilege of the intellectual part of the soul. In Descartes, soul now means "rational mind." In his work on the *Passions*, Descartes explicitly refers

2. Cf. the "Fifth Responses" in the *Meditations*, AT VII 230, CSM II 161.

back to his anatomy and physiology of blood circulation in his earlier *Discourse on Method*, where he also relies on animal spirits when presenting his research project of natural science (AT VI 54, CSM I 138, part 5). Hence *The Passions of the Soul* does not in principle deviate from the program of the *Discourse.*

In Part 5 of the *Discourse*, Descartes explicitly separates functions that are commonly attributed to the mind from the soul proper. Even speech can be found in animals as long as it is nothing but an indicator of some passions and, hence, can be imitated by machines.[3] While these functions can be compared with a clockwork, the soul cannot be reduced to matter (AT VI 58f., CSM I 140f). The human and the animal bodies are like robots that perform activities, including sense perception and communication. The mind comes in addition to that machine. Hence Gilbert Ryle's criticism that the mind is a mere "ghost in the machine."

What we find in the *Discourse* is the encounter of Descartes the scientist with Descartes the philosopher of knowledge. The early *Rules* had investigated the order of thinking for the sake of reliable interpretations of reality; the late *Passions* executed that in a paradigmatic way and showed to what extent methodical thinking can achieve scientific knowledge of one of the most insecure areas of research, human emotions. The *Discourse* links both efforts. It stresses method.

ON THE WAY TO SUBSTANCE DUALISM

Descartes entertained a notion of body, and of matter in general, that escapes the traditional terminology of substances. Descartes' famous *cogito ergo sum*, often translated as "I think therefore I am," identifies thinking as the essence of every *thing* that thinks. What is important for the notion of substance is that the content of what that thing is deliberately remains open. In a letter, Descartes claims that nothing material can be assuredly known to exist, whereas "the soul is a being or substance which is not at all corporeal, whose nature is solely to think" (AT I 353, CSM III 55). Descartes wavers between using terms such as "being," "substance," and "nature" (*estre, substance, nature*), which indicates that he is not committed to the professional philosophical terminology and concepts of his time. There is an incorporeal substance that exists by way of performing the thinking, and that is all that the mind can know.

Descartes' method approaches something like substance dualism in his further development of his theories. In the *Meditations on First Philosophy* he elaborates on the mental experiment of reducing the soul to mere thought. The major purpose of this text is to prove that the soul is immaterial (if not immortal). The reduction of soul to mind yields the certainty of "I am, I exist," which is necessarily true, whenever it is mentally conceived (AT VII 25, CSM II 17; 2nd med.). Once again we see the mind guaranteeing its own existence. After contrasting this existence with that of corporeal particulars and objects, Descartes pronounces that "I am, then, in the strict sense only a thing that thinks" (AT VII 27, CSM II 18). In the sixth meditation, Descartes distinguishes material objects from mind and stresses:

> I have a clear and distinct idea of myself, in so far as I am simply a thinking, non-extended thing (*res cogitans, non extensa*); and on the other hand I have a distinct idea of body, in so far as this is simply an extended, non-thinking thing (*res extensa, non cogitans*). (AT VII 78, CSM II 54)

This talk of thinking thing vs. extended thing (*res cogitans* vs. *res extensa*) suggests a clear dualism of

3. It sounds like an anticipation of John Searle's "Chinese Room": exchanging signs does not entail thinking (See Chapter 3).

mind and body. They are mutually exclusive substances that appear to make up the world. At this point, the fourth objection in the *Meditations*, raised by Antoine Arnauld (1612-1694), should be taken into account. Arnauld surmises that Descartes is either siding with Platonists who hold that the soul is the only constituent of a human being and that uses the body as a tool, or he is offering a traditional abstraction as geometers do who abstract figures from complex reality (AT VII 203f., CSM II 143). Platonists tend to deny dignity of material things and see all reality as results of spirit; geometers deal with mere abstractions (as anyone knows who tries to draw a perfect circle). In both cases the dualism would be dissolved. In reply, Descartes admits that this interpretation is possible but insists that the real distinction of mind from body is the result of attentive meditation (AT VII 228f., CSM II 160f).

RESHAPING THE CONCEPT OF SUBSTANCE

As pointed out repeatedly, Descartes is working with and around a traditional philosophical terminology while trying to escape it. Therefore, it is worth seeing how he defines "substance" in his *Principles of Philosophy*. One interpretation is that substance means "independent existence" and hence applies only to God who is defined as perfect and not dependent on anything. However, in the material world we learn about substances through the properties that appear to us. We don't see a lake as a substance; what we see is the shiny surface of water, surrounded by a shore, which leads us to perceiving the lake. The "principal attributes" of body and mind are notably extension and thinking, respectively (AT VIII 24f., CSM I 210f., sections 51-53). Descartes was careful not to jump to conclusions about the actual existence of material substances separate from their attributes. Hence he uses the imprecise word "thing" when referring to himself as essentially a thinking thing. The Latin term is *res*. Like "thing" in modern English, *res* has no ontological claim whatsoever, that is, when we say "thing" we avoid explaining what we mean and whether it is real. It is the "something" that language can point out without saying what it is.[4]

We may conclude that Descartes was aware of the temptation to present mind and body as competing and cooperating substances and he tried to escape the dualism, not only because any dualism is in need of some mediation, as the involvement of animal spirits proves, but also and foremost because of its explanatory deficits. On the one hand, his view appears to embrace the dualism that comes with inherited language (for instance from Platonism and Aristotelianism). On the other hand, if the philosophical problem of mind is that of understanding human knowledge, then understanding must be accessible to material beings and not within the realm of the immaterial. Therefore, Ryle was right to believe that Descartes fundamentally missed the task of understanding the mind.

To summarize the main points of the role of Descartes at the origin of modern philosophy of mind and specifically of substance dualism: Descartes aimed initially at proving that the human soul is immaterial (as Christian doctrine teaches); for that purpose he emphasized the certainty of rational thinking and its independence from body and material objects. This led him to the (still debated) question of how the mind can work with the body in the process of sense perceptions, feelings, etc. His response engaged the theory of "animal spirits," tenuous bodies that shuttle between the mind and the organs. As a consequence, he explained great deal of intellectual functions (perceptions, emotions, etc.) in purely physical terms. At the same time he underlined the immateriality of thinking. In

---

4. It is worth noting, perhaps, that the Latin version of the famous statement in the *Discourse* "From this I knew I was a substance …" modified "substance" by adding "any some thing or substance." Thus the author signaled that he was departing from traditional understanding of substance to a generic "something" (AT VI 558: "rem quondam sive substantiam").

traditional philosophical terminology, this amounted to the theory of two totally distinct substances: mind and body. However, it should be noted that Descartes undermined the concept of substance and reduced it to something deliberately vague. Therefore, philosophers who cling to the notion of substance as a reality will find substance dualism in Descartes; others, who focus on his attempts at explaining mental operations like perceptions and feelings in corporeal terms, will find him to be a proponent of physicalism.

REFERENCES

Adam, Charles and Paul Tannery, eds. 1964-1976. *Oeuvres de Descartes*. Paris: Vrin.

Campanella, Tommaso. 1999. *Compendio di filosofia della natura*, eds. Germana Ernst and Paolo Ponzio, sect. 61, 222. Santarcangelo di Romagna: Rusconi.

Cottingham, John G., Robert Stoothoff, Dugald Murdoch, and Anthony Kenny, trans. 1985-1991. *The Philosophical Writings of Descartes*, 3 vols. Cambridge: Cambridge University Press.

Ryle, Gilbert. 1949. *The Concept of Mind*. London/New York: Hutchinson's University Library: 11-16.

Sepper, Denis L. 2016. "Animal Spirits." In *The Cambridge Descartes Lexicon*, ed. Lawrence Nolan, 26-28. New York: Cambridge University Press.

FURTHER READING

Ariew, Roger. 2011. *Descartes among the Scholastics*. Leiden/Boston: Brill.

Cottingham, John. 1992. "Cartesian Dualism: Theology, Metaphysics, and Science." In *The Cambridge Companion to Descartes*, ed. John Cottingham, 236-57. Cambridge: Cambridge University Press.

Hassing, Richard F. 2015. *Cartesian Psychophysics and the Whole Nature of Man: On Descartes's Passions of the Soul*. Lanham: Lexington Books.

Markie, Peter. 1992. "The Cogito and Its Importance." In *The Cambridge Companion to Descartes*, ed. John Cottingham, 140-73. Cambridge: Cambridge University Press.

Ruler, Han van. 1999. "'Something, I Know Not What'. The Concept of Substance in Early Modern Thought." In *Between Demonstration and Imagination: Essays in the History of Science and Philosophy Presented to John D. North*, eds. Lodi Nauta and Arjo Vanderjagt, 365-93. Leiden: Brill.

Specht, Rainer. 1966. *Commercium mentis et corporis. Über Kausalvorstellungen im Cartesianismus*. Stuttgart-Bad Cannstatt: Frommann-Holzboog.

Voss, Stephen. 1993. "Simplicity and the Seat of the Soul." In *Essays on the Philosophy and Science of René Descartes*, ed. Stephen Voss, 128-41. New York: Oxford University Press.

CHAPTER 2.

MATERIALISM AND BEHAVIORISM

HEATHER SALAZAR

INTRODUCTION

In stark contrast to Cartesian substance dualism is materialism. Materialism denies the existence of a "mind" as an entity separate from the body. According to materialism, the concept of "mind" is a relic of the past from before a time of scientific understanding and when used today is only properly shorthand for "brain" or "behavior." Materialism therefore implies that: 1. There are no pure minds or souls in Heaven, Hell, or any such kind of afterlife after bodily death; 2. There are no spirits or immaterial essences, and therefore spiritual and self-transformative practices that purport to move people beyond their bodies, brains, and behaviors are absurd; and 3. Reincarnation and switching bodies (made famous in movies such as *Switching Places*, *Freaky Friday*, and *Big*) are nonsense. A mind just is a body or a body's behaviors; without a body a mind cannot exist.

Consider the movie *Big*. In it, a kid named Josh makes a wish to be "big" during an eerie encounter with a fortune-telling machine at a state fair. When he wakes, he is a 35-year-old adult and is unrecognizable to his mom. He convinces his best friend that he really is Josh and his best friend helps him to get a job and an apartment. Nevertheless, he cannot manage to grow emotionally enough to inhabit his new world. He frustrates his close female friend who cannot understand why he does not want to be romantic with her. According to the standard interpretation of stories like *Big*, a person's mind contains memories, love, fears, and so on. This is what constitutes the core of who a person really is. The mind is immaterial and cannot be seen; it can only be experienced by the person whose mind it is. But a person's mind is also connected to a body, which enables the person to communicate and interact with others in the world. Some bodies have minds (like other people) and some do not (like rocks). A body is incidental to a person's selfhood; it is just a house for the mind. So it is possible that a body can age and have the same mind. And this is what happens to Josh. Eventually, Josh finds the strange fortune-telling machine and wishes to be a boy again, and he re-enters his kid-body, now with the knowledge and wisdom he gained in his transformative journey.

Big is a fantasy, but it trades on common beliefs about what a person is (an immaterial mind) and what a body is (a material house for a mind which is incidental to a person's true identity). Note that if dualism is false and the body and mind are not two, but one, as materialism claims, then a person could not have the same mind in a vastly different body (or even in a slightly altered body). This is because every change in the memories, emotions, and experiences of a person would not take place in an immaterial mind, but rather would be translatable to talk of the body, the interactions of the body with the world, or as many materialists claim, talk of the brain.

Take what it would mean in *Big* for Josh to change according to such a materialist understanding. Imagine that it is possible to induce rapid aging in a person through an entirely physical process (say, the taking of a pill that speeds up a person's metabolism and turnover of bodily cells), such that overnight Josh ages by ten years. Even then, the turnover of those cells would have changed his mind just as much as it changed his body. But if his mind is identical and reducible to his brain, then his mind would (of logical necessity) be changed just as much as his body. This is evident through Leibniz's Law (also called the "indiscernibility of identicals"), which is a metaphysical truth that simply states that if something is identical to something else it must be identical in every way (or else it would not be the *same* object, but merely a *similar* object). That means Josh's mind would no longer be that of a boy; rather, he would have the mind of a man. Romantic desires would no longer be foreign to him (as they are in the movie) because the biological chemicals, such as testosterone, that are responsible for aging him into a man with a beard are the same chemicals that are responsible for creating sex drives. His biochemistry would be changed and so would his energy levels and emotions. Furthermore, his brain mass would be larger, since a person's brain grows in the process of aging from childhood to adulthood. That additional brain mass would entail not only different biochemicals, but also more and differently connected neurons. Those are the same neurons and connections, materialists claim, that are responsible for the development of concepts, language, understanding, and so on. So if Josh woke up with his body transformed into a man, then his mind would be changed just as much. He could not possibly wake up with the same mind he had as a boy, according to a materialist.

The story of *Big* is not just impossible; it is nonsense. The fact that people easily make sense of the story and readily suspend their disbelief shows just how deeply ingrained dualist assumptions of the body and mind are. Our ignorance and ability to be misled by fantasies, however, does not show that materialism is false. Instead, the materialist will state, it shows we are gullible and that intuition is not a reliable guide to the truth. If we were more sophisticated in our ability to grasp reality, *Big* would seem unbelievable and incomprehensible.

There are many different versions of materialism and behaviorism. This chapter will introduce some of the most common motivations for embracing it and some of the most important historical developments of it.

EMPIRICISM AND SCIENCE AS REPLACEMENT FOR GOD

The scientific revolution began in the mid-sixteenth century and the progress of science throughout the nineteenth century made science a proven method of quick advancement for knowledge. Some philosophers, such as David Hume (1711-1796), argued that people should "reject every system ... however subtle or ingenious, which is not founded on fact and observation" (Hume [1751] 1998). He and those who agree are called empiricists. Rene Descartes (1596-1650) (who argued for substance dualism) and John Locke (1632-1704) had philosophical theories that tried to forward philosophical views within science, then called mechanical philosophy, which sought to find explanations that were subject to physical laws. Whereas Descartes was a rationalist, relying on principle, Locke was an empiricist and relied on experience (constituting evidence). Both Descartes and Locke had to prove that their theories were consistent with God and the religion of the time (which in Europe was Christianity); however, later theorists either left God completely out of the picture or tried to show from a theoretical basis that there still was a place for God in science.

Some of the important foundations of science, such as the closure principle and the primacy of the empirical over the theoretical, were prominent in philosophy, as well. In the sciences, experiments and theories rely centrally on the closure principle, which states that material objects have causes and effects that are locatable in the physical world. Without this principle, there would be no reason to do scientific research. Instead of claiming that the cause of a disease is a virus, we could just as easily claim that it is caused by God's wrath or a demonic force. This slowly caused people to rethink their ideas of the existence of God. If God was no longer needed to explain the things that we experience in the world—if science could do it completely without the use of God—then why do we need to believe in the existence of God?

An empiricist will readily point out that you cannot see God, nor can see your mind. You may be able to see someone else's brain if you witness a surgeon operating on someone, but you cannot see anyone's mind, including your own. And according to the principle of closure, something that is immaterial cannot affect something that is material, so the brain or other physical things are more properly the cause of our actions, not some mystical immaterial substance of the mind.

The principle of Ockham's Razor—named after William of Ockham (1285-1347), a philosopher from the middle ages—states that when something of a different kind (in this case, immaterial things) is not needed to explain something else (material things), then it can be eliminated. Favored in the sciences, Ockham's Razor is an explanatory principle of parsimony, and it gave philosophers a justification to remove God and other items that could not be seen (like minds) from their ontological status as real (separate) objects. Instead, talk of minds and mental events, such as thoughts and feelings, are simply shorthand expressions for processes in the body and world that science helps people to understand. It is therefore reasonable, they thought, that either minds really are just bodies or else minds do not exist. Ockham's Razor became the battle-cry of the new materialist brand of philosophers, scientists, and psychologists in the modern era and even today.

MATERIALISM

Some philosophers who worked in the same time period as Descartes and Locke, such as Thomas Hobbes (1588-1679), began to follow a theory generally called materialism or physicalism, which states that all there is in the world and in us is material, and there is nothing immaterial. The mind had historically been conceived as immaterial with immaterial properties, such as thinking, believing, and desiring. Hobbes, however, insisted that the mind—and even God—must be material. When I think of a cat and you think of a cat, we think of the same concept (we assume), but how can we *know* that, and communicate with confidence, when there is nothing physical in the thought? How is it the case that we can ever verify that we are thinking of the same thing? Under materialism, if there is no such thing as an immaterial mind then what was previously called "thinking" must instead be explained by the body, the interactions of the body in the world, or more simply in modern materialism, the neurological firings of the brain. What we think of as thinking is an action of the body, and what we think of when we think of concepts such as "cat" is anchored in the material world of sense perception.

Type identity is a materialist theory that asserts that all mental states are identical to certain types of physical states. Contemporary proponents J. J. C. Smart (1920-2012) and U. T. Place (1924-2000) explained that science will reveal to us through experiments which kinds of mental states are equivalent to which kinds of physical processes in the brain. Note that a correlation between two kinds of states does not show that they are identical: a mental one of love and a physical one of more available serotonin in the brain, for example. Also, a physical event under type identity cannot be said to cause a mental one. Being hugged by someone does not cause a feeling happiness; rather it is an example of a physical action that causes certain nerves in the skin to send signals to the brain and create a sequence of firing that is identical to a feeling of happiness. Both correlation and causation assume that there are two events of different kinds that are related. Under materialism, there is just one kind of thing, so while it may appear that a mental and a physical event are related, the mental event is identical to the physical event. It is important to refrain from these errors when speaking about materialism.

Brain scans reveal the physical processes that happen in the brain when people commonly experience seemingly mental events, giving credence to the type identity theorist's assertion that mental and brain events are just the same thing. A well-known example is that of the experience of pain, a kind of mental event that appears to be an immaterial feeling. The type identity theorist states that pain just is the completely physical event of C-fibers firing in the brain. When C-fibers fire, a person is in pain. Sometimes a person may not be fully aware of the pain they have, say, for example, if their attention is elsewhere or if another neurological process is covering up a subjective experience of pain. Imagine a person who gets struck in the head by a large rock. He is in fact injured and C-fibers fire in the brain, but then the person becomes unconscious. That is not to say he is not in pain; he is just unaware of it. Or say that a person gets attacked by a shark in the ocean and succeeds in fending it off. She is bleeding and is injured, but the ocean is so cold that her extremities are numb. In this case, there is a different physical process that is either postponing or covering up C-fibers firing, and therefore her experience of pain will be delayed until she is out of the cold ocean.

There have been numerous attacks against type identity theory that are so successful that many identity theorists have changed their account. One of the most devastating objections is based on the observation that different kinds of brains can realize pain. Animals surely experience pain like we do, but most animals have dramatically different brains, connections, and biochemicals than we do, so mental events like pain cannot be categorically reduced to a particular human brain kind of event. Hilary Putnam (1926-2016) astutely argued that this observation, called the multiple realizability of the mental, should lead us to abandon any supposed identity of kinds between the mental and the physical (Putnam 1967). Any account of mental events must explain how similar mental events appear to take place across a wide range of physical beings. We might even imagine beings from a distant planet who are silicone-based instead of carbon-based that also experience pain even though their systems have no physical similarities whatsoever to human brains and neurological events. This argument has led many to embrace a different account of the identity or reduction of the mental to the physical. In order to avoid this criticism, for example, token identity theories purport that all mental events reduce to a physical brain state, yet claim the identity is not necessarily instantiated by the same or similar brain states between people, or even within a single person at various times. Expositions of this theory vary and can often cross into other theories of mind, such as functionalism (see Chapter 3) and property dualism (see Chapter 4), so they will not be discussed here.

* Wiki: Putnam noted that the multiple realizability of pain entails that, contrary to type-identity theory, pain's not identical to C-fibre firing. More generally, MR shows that psychological attributes are not the same as physical attributes. Pain is...

[right margin handwritten:] attributes, rather, are disjunctions (a cluster of disjuncts of requisite attributes.)

Despite most theorists' discouragement of the arguments against type identity theory, there is a more radical materialist theory that embraces even more counterintuitive conclusions. Instead of taking on the explanatory burden of connecting the identity of mental and brain events, these theorists claim that everything is purely physical. There are no thoughts, no emotions, no minds. Everything is just an effect of brain and other physical processes. This kind of materialism is called eliminative materialism or reductive materialism because it states not only that the mind and the world should be explained consistently and within science as Descartes and Locke agreed, or that the mind should be seen as part of the physical realm as the type identity theorists do, but that there simply is no mind. Contemporary proponents of eliminative materialism Paul Churchland and Patricia Churchland explain our perceptions of the world according to neurology. An eliminative materialist would say that the feeling of pain is an illusion. We have become habituated to call certain things pain when at bottom there are only physical events happening. In discussions with the Dalai Lama, Patricia Churchland claims that she cannot say she even has the emotion of love toward her own child (because love is an illusion) and the beliefs of ordinary people who say there are such things as love and other emotions are false (Houshmand, Livingston, and Wallace 1999). Folk psychology, the theory of mind that embraces intuitions by the "common folk" who are uneducated about science, is merely a convenient myth.

Eliminative materialism is the most extreme view opposing substance dualism. The eliminative materialist truly eliminates the existence of minds, and with them, all of the features of mentality. They reject experiences, thoughts, and even actions. Therefore, although eliminative materialism explains everything within a scientific framework, it does so at the great cost of our intuitions, thoughts, feelings, and selves. Indeed, it eliminates most of what a theory of mind intends to understand. Many philosophers claim that Ockham's Razor has gone too far if most of what we intended to explain gets dismissed entirely. An account of the mind that brings back more of the features of normal life and explains those within a scientific framework is preferable to preserve the life and meaning of what people think, do, and say.

BEHAVIORISM AND THE LOGICAL POSITIVISTS

In the empiricist tradition, a different movement attempted to situate the mind within the realm of the material world, not through the identity of the two but through the explanation of the mind completely in terms of physical behaviors and events. Logical behaviorism claims that mental events (like pain) are to be understood as a set of behaviors (saying "ouch," screaming, or cringing after being hit). In this way, pain is entirely explainable within a concrete scientific framework that can be observed and communicated clearly between all beings.

The logical positivists (spanning from the Vienna Circle in 1922 through the 1950s in the United States) thought that if they could mimic the methods of the sciences that philosophical advances would also be imminent. Those such as Otto Neurath (1882-1945) and Rudolph Carnap (1891-1970) performed rigorous analyses to show that the mind and other non-observable and non-scientifically verifiable objects did not exist, and that those things we thought were immaterial could be constructed from completely material objects and processes. Some argued that all talk of immaterial objects or processes should be eliminated from our language. Their impact was tremendous and the terrain of Western philosophy shifted toward philosophy of language throughout the twentieth century. The period of logical positivism is also known as "the linguistic turn" (of the century). Some of the most important philosophers of the twentieth century, Ludwig Wittgenstein (1889-1951) and W. V. O. Quine (1908-2000), were closely aligned with the Vienna Circle and logical positivism.

The logical positivists appeared to have a solution for the dilemma concerning the meaning of what people say and the integration of the mental within the physical. Instead of rendering everything involving the mental illusory or false, mental talk can be translated and should be translated into talk of behavior. The mind therefore becomes encapsulated within the realm of action. The argument goes like this: we do not need to eliminate all talk of our minds or our thoughts, and we do not need to say that all things involving such subjects are false. It is just that the meanings of all of those words and thoughts are not what they seem at first. What these words really are is a kind of shorthand for things that are all empirically observable, and most importantly, our behaviors. After all, we cannot see our thoughts and it seems like what we have always really meant by our talk of the mental we have created from observations of behavior. When I say, "Mom is angry," what I mean is that she is acting in such and such a way, not smiling, furrowing her eyebrows, not talking much, and so on. In this way, many of the things that we say come out true, and they all rely on empirical evidence—the evidence that we have always been gathering from the behavior of people. According to the logical behaviorist, if mental talk cannot be translated into behavior talk, then that particular mental talk is meaningless, just like Lewis Carroll's nonsense poem "Jabberwocky." The poem sounds grammatical and it resembles real words: "Twas bryllyg, and the slythy toves," it begins (Carroll and Tenniel 1872). People often have interpretations and emotional reactions to it, but it does not mean anything. Logical behaviorists believed poetry, art, and much of literature fell into this camp. It was entertaining but meaningless.

The logical behaviorists soon became overrun by possibly the most decisive objections in the history of philosophy. Whereas most philosophical positions refine themselves and carry more or fewer adherents, logical positivism and logical behaviorism had such devastating objections of inconsistency leveled against them that adhering to them became nearly impossible. There are two theoretical objections that were particularly damaging for logical behaviorism. The first depends on the principle of verificationism. Many of the logical positivists, including Carl Hempel (1905-1997), held a theory whereby all truths relied on their verification, either analytically (in virtue of their meanings, or by definition) or synthetically (not in virtue of their meanings, which, for Hempel indicated that they were true by experience) (Hempel 1980). Rudolph Carnap, though a member of the Vienna Circle, realized that verification was too stringent a demand to be met by any proposition, and he spent a good portion of his philosophical career trying out different criteria to rescue the theory from the criticism. As argued by Hilary Putnam, the principle of verification itself could not be verified and it was therefore "self-refuting" (Putnam 1983). Second, behaviorists were unable to provide the necessary and sufficient behavioral conditions required for translating talk about minds into talk about behaviors. In fact, Peter Geach (1916-2013) gave an objection to logical behaviorism that eliminated any kind of definition of beliefs or other mental states purely in terms of behaviors. Everything that a person does, or is disposed to do, depends on the person's beliefs and desires, so defining one belief in terms of certain actions just prolongs the problem of defining it, since the actions used to define it will make reference to yet other beliefs and desires. The account is therefore circular (Geach 1957, 8).

Another objection argues that behavior is both unnecessary and insufficient to account for what people mean by their use of mental concepts. The success of this objection affects the strong version of logical behaviorism (and usually the view to which people refer) which states that there are necessary and sufficient conditions within behavior to define mentality. To refute this view, focusing on the sufficiency of the behavior, a critic must find cases where there is behavior that mimics the existence of minds but where there is no mind. Ned Block, for example, said that puppets controlled via radio links by other minds outside the puppet's hollow body would mimic a mind working but is not a mind working (Block 1981). To refute the other side, that behavior is necessary for mentality, which could be seen as a weaker form of behaviorism if accepted without the sufficiency condition, the critic needs to find examples where there is thinking going on, but without the behavior. This is more difficult. Disembodied minds or thinking objects, if they exist, could constitute counterexamples. Hilary Putnam argued that we can imagine a world in which people experience pain but are conditioned to disguise their pain behaviors (Putnam 1963). Our ability to coherently think of such a world shows that pain is not conceptually and necessarily tied to behaviors, even if in our world we most often experience them contingently connected (see Chapter 5). Ludwig Wittgenstein, regarded as a champion for the logical positivists and the behaviorists, himself eventually turned away from a behaviorist-like theory to a theory that relied on thoughts as separate and independent from our descriptions of them.

CONCLUSION

Today, materialist and behaviorist views enjoy prominence in the sciences, but not in philosophy. Biologists and neuroscientists are working hard to uncover the mysteries of behavior and the brain. Each time they learn more information, they help build a better basis for a purely empirical philosophy of mind. But empirical research alone will never be sufficient to ground a materialist or behaviorist theory of mind. Both the radical theory of eliminativism (which intends to show that the mind does not exist) and non-reductive identity theories (which propose that mental events are always the same as physical events) still require persuasive philosophical arguments to show that minds are redundant or unnecessary in our ontology. Scientists themselves rely on self-reports of feelings and thoughts even while they conduct studies attempting to show that the mind can be reduced to the brain. An evolution in our ways of studying the body and the brain that do not rely on self-reports of feelings and thoughts seems a long way off.

The problem is that evidence of the workings of the body and brain, no matter how advanced, can never in itself establish a definite reduction of the mind to the body and the brain. Science alone cannot demonstrate the equivalence of the mind to the body or brain. Thus far, Ockham's Razor has not yet successfully shaved off the necessity of talk about minds for most philosophers. One day, an evolution in human ways of relating to ourselves and each other may rely less on feelings and thoughts and more on reactions and behaviors. Perhaps, it may be observed, the human condition was once like that, more instinctual in origin. Even if this is true, observations of the origin of human life do not indicate that our current human condition is entirely material. Some may argue that an evolution towards reliance on an immaterial mind marks progress in our species. Others may argue that the evolution of a seemingly immaterial mind shows the sophistication of brain. The debate will likely continue until talk of immaterial minds appears to be unnecessary.

REFERENCES

Block, Ned. 1981. "Troubles with Functionalism." In *Minnesota Studies in the Philosophy of Science IX*, ed. C. Wade Savage, 261-325. Minneapolis: University of Minnesota Press.

Carroll, Lewis and John Tenniel. 1872. *Through the Looking-Glass: And What Alice Found There*. London: Macmillan.

Geach, Peter. 1957. *Mental Acts: Their Content and Their Objects*. London: Routledge & Kegan Paul.

Hempel, Carl. 1980. "The Logical Analysis of Psychology." In *Readings in Philosophy of Psychology*, ed. Ned Block, 1-14. Cambridge: Harvard University Press.

Houshmand, Zara, Robert Livingston, and B. Alan Wallace, eds. 1999. *Consciousness at the Crossroads: Conversations with the Dalai Lama on Brain Science and Buddhism*. Ithaca: Snow Lion Publications.

Hume, David. (1751) 1998. *An Enquiry Concerning the Principles of Morals*, ed. Tom L. Beauchamp, 1.10. Oxford: Oxford University Press.

Putnam, Hilary. 1983. "Philosophers and Human Understanding." In *Realism and Reason: Philosophical Papers, Vol. 3*, 184-204. Cambridge: Cambridge University Press.

Putnam, Hilary. 1967. "Psychological Predicates." In *Art, Mind, and Religion*, eds. W. H. Capitan and D. D. Merrill, 37-48. Pittsburgh: University of Pittsburgh Press.

Putnam, Hilary. 1963. "Brains and Behaviour." In *Analytical Philosophy*, ed. R. J. Butler, 1-19. Malden, MA: Wiley Blackwell.

FURTHER READING

Churchland, Paul. 1989. *A Neurocomputational Perspective*. Cambridge, MA: MIT Press.

Churchland, Patricia. 1986. *Neurophilosophy: Toward a Unified Science of the Mind/Brain*. Cambridge, MA: MIT Press.

Hempel, Carl. 1966. *Philosophy of Natural Science*. Englewood Cliffs, NJ: Prentice-Hall.

Putnam, Hilary. 1975. *Mind, Language and Reality: Philosophical Papers, Vol. 2*. Cambridge: Cambridge University Press.

Ryle, Gilbert. 1949. *The Concept of Mind*. London: Hutchison.

Quine, W. V. O. 1966. "On Mental Entities." In *The Ways of Paradox*. Random House.

Searle, John. 1997. *The Mystery of Consciousness*. New York: The New York Review of Books.

Sellars, Wilfrid. 1956. "Empiricism and the Philosophy of Mind." In *The Foundations of Science and the Concepts of Psychology and Psychoanalysis: Minnesota Studies in the Philosophy of Science* (Volume 1), eds. Herbert Feigl and Michael Scriven, 253-329. Minneapolis: University of Minnesota Press.

Smart, J. J. C. 1959. "Sensations and Brain Processes." *Philosophical Review* 68 (April): 141-156.

Stich, Stephen. 1983. *From Folk Psychology to Cognitive Science*. Cambridge, MA: MIT Press.

CHAPTER 3.

FUNCTIONALISM

JASON NEWMAN

INTRODUCTION: TWO MONSTERS WE MUST AVOID

While passing through the Strait of Messina, between mainland Italy and the isle of Sicily, Homer has Odysseus come upon two monsters, Scylla and Charybdis, one on either side of the strait. If Odysseus is to pass through the strait, he must choose between two very unhappy options; for if he averts one along the way, he will move in the other's monstrous reach. On the one side is roaring Charybdis, who would surely blot out—as if by colossal whirlpool—Odysseus's entire ship. (Have you ever been faced with an option so bad that you cannot believe you have to seriously consider it? Well, this is Odysseus's bleak situation.) On the other side of the strait, things fare little better for Odysseus and his war-weary crew: we have vicious Scylla, who only by comparison to Charybdis, looks like the right choice. The ship makes it through, Homer tells us, minus those who were snatched from the ship's deck and eaten alive. Six are taken, we are told, one for each of Scylla's heads. By comparison only, indeed.

In this chapter we consider the theory of mind known as functionalism, the view that minds are really functional systems like the computing systems we rely on every day, only much more complex. The functionalist claims to sail a middle path between materialism (discussed in Chapter 2), or the joint thesis that minds are brains and mental states are brain states, and behaviorism (also discussed in Chapter 2), or the thesis that mental states are behavioural states or dispositions to behave in certain ways.

AVOIDING MATERIALISM

One the one side we have materialism, which we must avoid because there appears to be no strict identity between mental states and brain states. Even though human Freya is different than a wild rabbit in many interesting ways, we think they can both be in physical pain. Suppose that while restringing her guitar, Freya lodges a rogue metal splinter off the D string in the top of her ring finger. She winces in pain. Physiologically and neurologically, a lot happened—from the tissue damage caused by the metal splinter, to Freya's finally wincing from the sensation. But it only took milliseconds.

Now suppose that while out foraging and hopping about, the wild rabbit mishops on the prickly side of a pinecone. The rabbit cries out a bit, winks hard, and hops off fast. A very similar physiological and neurological chain of events no doubt transpired from the mishop on the pinecone to hopping off fast in pain. But as interestingly similar as the wild rabbit's brain is to human Freya's, it is not plausible to think that both Freya and the wild rabbit entered into the same brain state. We do want to say they entered into the same *mental* state, however. That is, they were both in pain. Since the same pain state can be realized in multiple kinds of brains, we can say that mental states like pain are multiply realizable. This is bad news for the materialist; it looks like brain states and mental states come apart.

AVOIDING BEHAVIORISM

Now we look bleary-eyed in the direction of behaviorism. But here, too, we find a suspicious identity claim—this time between mental states, like Freya's belief that her house is gray, and behavioral states or dispositions to behave in certain circumstances. For example, if Freya were asked what color her house is, she would be disposed to answer, "Gray." But just as with mental states and brain states, Freya's believing that her Colonial-period house is painted the original gray from when the house was first built and painted in 1810, and her dispositions to behave accordingly, come apart, showing that they could not be identical.

Suppose Freya wants to throw a housewarming party for herself and includes a colorful direction in the invitation that hers is the "only big gray Colonial on Jones St. Can't miss it." We say that Freya would not sincerely include such a thing if she did not believe it to be true. And we have no reason to suspect she is lying. We can go further. We want to say that it is her belief that her Colonial is big, is gray, and the only one like it on Jones Street that causes her, at least in part, to include that direction in the invitation. But if it is her mental state (her belief) that caused her behavior, then the mental state and the behavioral state (her including the colorful direction in the invitation) cannot be strictly identical.

Freya might very well have been disposed to give just such a colorful direction to her home, given her beliefs, as the behaviorist would predict; and this disposition might even come with believing the things Freya does. But if we want to refer to Freya's beliefs in our explanation of her behavior—and this is the sort of thing we do when we say our beliefs and other mental states cause our behavior—then we must hold that they are distinct, since otherwise our causal explanation would be viciously circular.

It would be circular because the thing to be explained, her Colonial-describing behavior, is the same thing as the thing that is supposed to causally explain it, her Colonial-descriptive beliefs; and the circle would be vicious because nothing would ever really get explained. So the behaviorist, like the materialist, seems to see an identity where there is none.

NO TURNING BACK: THE MIND IS NATURAL

The goal is to formulate an alternative to the above two theories of mind that nevertheless both make a promise worth making: to treat the mind as something wholly a part of the natural world. From the failures of materialism and behaviorism, we must not turn back to a problematic Cartesian dualist view of mind and matter (discussed in Chapter 1), where it again would become utterly mysterious how Freya's beliefs about how her Colonial looks could possibly influence her physical behavior, since her beliefs and physical behavior exist on different planes of existence, as it were. But there is a third way to view beliefs like Freya's.

FUNCTIONALISM AS THE MIDDLE PATH

Our way between the two monsters is to take seriously the perhaps dangerous idea that minds really are computing machines. In England, Alan Turing (1912-1954) laid the groundwork for such an idea with his monumental work on the nature of computing machines and intelligence (1936, 230-265; 1950, 433-460). Turing was able to conceive of a computing machine so powerful that it could successfully perform any computable function a human being could be said to carry out, whether consciously, as in the math classroom, or at the subconscious level, as in the many computations involved in navigating from one side to the other of one's room.

A Turing machine, as it came to be called, is an abstract computer model designed with the purpose of illustrating the limits of computability. Thinking creatures like human beings, of course, are not abstract things. Turing machines are not themselves thinking machines, but insofar as thinking states can be coherently understood as computational states, a Turing machine or Turing machine-inspired model should provide an illuminating account of the mind.

Turing's ideas were developed in the United States by philosopher Hilary Putnam (1926-2016). Functionalism treats minds as natural phenomena contra Cartesian dualism; mental states, like pain, as multiply realizable, contra materialism; and mental states as causes of behavior, contra behaviorism. In its simple form, it is the joint thesis that the mind is a functional system, kind of like an operating system of a computer, and mental states like beliefs, desires, and perceptual experiences are really just functional states, kind of like inputs and outputs in that operating system. Indeed, often this simple version of functionalism is known as "machine" or "input-output functionalism" to highlight just those mechanical features of the theory.

NOTHING'S SHOCKING: THE FUNCTIONALIST MIND IS A NATURAL MIND

The functionalist says if we conceive of mental stuff in this way—namely, as fundamentally inputs and outputs in a complex, but wholly natural system—then we get to observe the reality of the mind, and the reality of our mental lives. We get to avoid any genuine worries about mental stuff being too spooky, or about how it could possibly interact with material stuff, as one might genuinely worry on a Cartesian dualist theory of mind, where we are asked to construe mental stuff and material stuff as fundamentally two kinds of substances. With functionalism, the how-possible question about interaction between the mental and material simply does not arise, no more than it would for the software and hardware interaction in computers, respectively. So, on the functionalist picture of the mind, the mysterious fog is lifted, and the way is clear.

MULTIPLE REALIZABILITY

Let us use a thought experiment of our own to illustrate the functionalist's theory of mind. Imagine Freya cooks a warm Sunday breakfast for herself and sits on a patio table in the spring sun to enjoy it. Freya's belief that "my tofu scramble is on the table before me" is to be understood roughly like this: as the OUTPUT of one mental state, her seeing her breakfast on the table before her, and as the

INPUT for others, including other beliefs Freya might have or come to have by deductive inference ("something is on the table before me," and so on and so forth) and behaviors (e.g., sticking a fork into that tofu scramble and scarfing it down). Note well: we have not mentioned anything here about the work Freya's sensory cortex or thalamus or the role the rods and cones in her retina are playing in getting her to believe what she does; her belief is identified only by its functional or causal role. This seems to imply that Freya's breakfast belief is multiply realizable, like pain is.

Recall our earlier discussion of the important difference between rabbit-brain stuff and human-brain stuff. Nevertheless, we wanted to say that both Freya and the wild rabbit could be in pain. We said pain, then, is multiply realizable. This is another way of saying that being in pain does not require any specific realization means, just some or other adequate means of realization. The point also strongly implies that the means of realization for Freya's breakfast belief, no less than her pain, need not be a brain state at all. This signals a major worry for the materialist. Since our beliefs, desires, and perceptual experiences are identified by their functional or causal role, the functionalist has no problem accounting for the multiple realizability of mental states.

REAL CAUSE: THE FUNCTIONALIST MIND CAUSES BEHAVIOR

Finally, we saw that our mental states cannot be counted as the causes of our behavior on a behaviorist view, since on that view of mind, mental states are nothing over and above our behavior (or, dispositions to behave in certain ways in certain circumstances). In an effort to disenchant the mind in general and individual minds in particular, and move mental states like beliefs and pain into scientific view, the behaviorist recoiled too far from spooky Cartesian dualism, leaving nothing in us to be the causes of our own behavior. The functionalist understands, like the behaviorist, that there is a close connection between our beliefs, desires, and pains, on the one hand, and our behavior, on the other. It is just that the connection is a functional, or causal, one, not one of identity. Since mental states (like Freya's belief that "my tofu scramble is on the table before me") are identified with their functional or causal role in the larger functional system of inputs and outputs, other mental states and behavioral states, the functionalist has no problem accounting for mental states playing a causal role in the explanations we give of our own behavior. On the functionalist theory of mind, mental states are real causes of behavior.

OBJECTIONS TO FUNCTIONALISM

Now that we have seen some of the major points in favor of the theory, let us have a look at some of the worries that have been raised against functionalism.

The Chinese Room

John Searle argues against a version of functionalism he calls "strong" artificial intelligence, or "strong AI" In "Minds, Brains and Programs," Searle develops a thought experiment designed to show that having the right inputs and outputs is not sufficient for having mental states, as the functionalist claims (1980). The specific issue concerns what is required to understand Chinese.

Imagine someone who does not understand Chinese is put in a room and tasked with sorting Chinese symbols in response to other Chinese symbols, according to purely formal rules given in an English-language manual. So, for example, one person can write some Chinese symbols on a card, place it in a basket on a conveyor belt which leads into and out from the little room you are in. Once you receive it, you look at the shape of the symbol, find it in the manual, and read which Chinese symbols to find in the other basket to send back out. Imagine further that you get very good at this manipulation of symbols, so good in fact that you can fool fluent Chinese speakers with the responses you give. To them, you function every bit like you understand Chinese. It appears, however, you have no true understanding at all. Therefore, Searle concludes, functioning in the right way is not sufficient for having mental states.

The functionalist has replied that, of course, as the thought experiment is described, the person in the room does not understand Chinese. But also as the case is described, the person in the room is just a piece of the whole functional system. Indeed, it is the system that functions to understand Chinese, not just one part. So it is the whole system, in this case, the whole room, including the person manipulating the symbols and the instruction manual (the "program"), that understands Chinese.

The Problem of Qualia

The splinter Freya picked up from her D string caused her a bit of pain, and perhaps more so for the behaviorist, as we saw earlier. One major worry for the functionalist is that there seems to be more to Freya's pain than its just being the putative cause of some pain-related behavior, where this cause is understood to be another mental state, presumably, not identified with pain at all. (Remember, the functionalist wishes to avoid the vicious circularity that plagued the behaviorist's explanations of behavior.)

There is an undeniable sensation to pain: it is something you feel. In fact, some might argue that at the conscious level, that is all there is to pain. Sure, there is the detection of tissue damage and the host physiological and neurological events transpiring, and yes, there is the pain-related behavior, too. However, we must not leave out of our explanation of pain the feel of pain. Philosophers call the feeling aspect of some mental states like pain fundamentally qualitative states. Other qualitative mental states might include experiences of colored objects, such as those a person with normal color vision has every day.

In seeing a Granny Smith apple in the basket on a dining room table, she has a visual experience as of a green object. But the functionalist can only talk about the experience in terms of the function or causal role it plays. So, for example, the functionalist can speak to Freya's green experience as being the cause of her belief that she sees a green apple in the basket. But the functionalist cannot speak to the feeling Freya (or any of us) has in seeing a ripe green Granny Smith. We think there is a corresponding feeling to color experiences like Freya's over and above whatever beliefs they might go on to cause us to have. Since mental states like pain and color experiences are identified solely by their functional role, the functionalist seems without the resources to account for these qualitative mental states.

The functionalist might reply by offering a treatment of qualia in terms of what such aspects of experience function to do for us. The vivid, ripe greenness of the Granny Smith functions to inform Freya about a source of food in a way that pulls her visual attention to it. Freya's color experiences allow her to form accurate beliefs about the objects in her immediate environment. It is certainly true that ordinary visual experience provide us with beautiful moments in our lives. However, they likely function to do much more besides. Likewise, it is more likely that there is a function for the qualitative or feeling aspects of some mental states, and that these aspects can be understood in terms of their functions, than it is that these aspects are free-floating above the causal order of things. So, the functionalist who wishes to try to account for qualia need not remain silent on the issue.

CONCLUSION

We have not considered all the possible objections to functionalism, nor have we considered more sophisticated versions of functionalism that aim to get around the more pernicious objections we have considered. The idea that minds really are kinds of computing machines is still very much alive and as controversial as ever. Taking that idea seriously means having to wrestle with a host of questions at the intersection of philosophy of mind, philosophy of action, and personal identity.

In what sense is Freya truly an *agent* of her own actions, if we merely cite a cold input to explain some behavior of hers? That is to say, how does Freya *avow* her own beliefs on a merely functionalist view? If minds are kinds of computers, then what does that make thinking creatures like Freya? Kinds of robots, albeit sophisticated ones? These and other difficult questions will need to be answered satisfactorily before many philosophers will be content with a functionalist theory of mind. For other philosophers, a start down the right path, away from Cartesian dualism and between the two terrors of materialism and behaviorism, has already been made.

REFERENCES

Putnam, Hilary. (1960) 1975. "Minds and Machines." Reprinted in *Mind, Language, and Reality*, 362-385. Cambridge: Cambridge University Press.

Searle, John. 1980. "Minds, Brains, and Programs." *Behavioral and Brain Sciences* 3(3): 417-457.

Turing, Alan, M. 1936. "On Computable Numbers, with an Application to the Entscheidungsproblem." *Proceedings of the London Mathematical Society* 42 (1): 230-265.

Turing, Alan, M. 1950. "Computing Machinery and Intelligence." *Mind* 49: 433-460.

FURTHER READING

Block, Ned. 1980a. *Readings in the Philosophy of Psychology, Volumes 1 and 2*. Cambridge, MA: Harvard University Press.

Block, Ned. 1980b. "Troubles With Functionalism." In Block 1980a, 268-305.

Gendler, Tamar. 2008. "Belief and Alief." *Journal of Philosophy* 105(10): 634-663.

Jackson, Frank. 1982. "Epiphenomenal Qualia." *Philosophical Quarterly* 32: 127-136.

Lewis, David. 1972. "Psychophysical and Theoretical Identifications." In Block 1980a, 207-215.

Lewis, David. 1980. "Mad Pain and Martian Pain." In Block 1980, 216-222.

Nagel, Thomas. 1974. "What Is It Like To Be a Bat?" *Philosophical Review* 83: 435-450.

Putnam, Hilary. 1963. "Brains and Behavior." Reprinted in Putnam 1975b, 325-341.

Putnam, Hilary. 1967. "The Nature of Mental States." Reprinted in Putnam 1975b, 429-440.

Putnam, Hilary. 1973. "Philosophy and our Mental Life." Reprinted in Putnam 1975b, 291-303.

Putnam, Hilary. 1975a. "The Meaning of 'Meaning.'" Reprinted in Putnam 1975b, 215-271.

Putnam, Hilary. 1975b. *Mind, Language, and Reality*. Cambridge: Cambridge University Press.

Shoemaker, Sydney. 1984. *Identity, Cause, and Mind*. Cambridge: Cambridge University Press.

Shoemaker, Sydney. 1996. *The First-Person Perspective and Other Essays*. Cambridge: Cambridge University Press.

CHAPTER 4.

PROPERTY DUALISM

ELLY VINTIADIS

INTRODUCTION

The first thing that usually comes to mind when one thinks of dualism is René Descartes' (1596-1650) substance dualism. However, there is another form of dualism, quite popular nowadays, which is called property dualism, a position which is sometimes associated with non-reductive physicalism.

Cartesian dualism posits two substances, or fundamental kinds of thing: material substance and immaterial thinking substance. These are two entirely different kinds of entities, although they interact with each other. According to property dualism, on the other hand, there is one fundamental kind of thing in the world—material substance—but it has two essentially different kinds of property: physical properties and mental properties. So for instance, a property dualist might claim that a material thing like a brain can have both physical properties (like weight and mass) and mental properties (such as having a particular belief or feeling a shooting pain), and that these two kinds of properties are entirely different in kind. Some philosophers subscribe to property dualism for all mental properties while others defend it only for conscious or "phenomenal" properties such as the feeling of pain or the taste of wine.[1] These latter properties give rise to what is known as the hard problem of consciousness: How do we explain the existence of consciousness in a material world?

Though these are both dualist views, they differ in fundamental ways. Property dualism was proposed as a position that has a number of advantages over substance dualism. One advantage is that, because it does not posit an immaterial mental substance, it is believed to be more scientific than Cartesian dualism and less religiously motivated. A second advantage is that it seems to avoid the problem of mental causation because it posits only one kind of substance; there is no communication between two different kinds of thing. And a third advantage is that, by maintaining the existence of distinctly mental properties, it does justice to our intuitions about the reality of the mind and its difference from the physical world. But to understand all this we need to take a step back.

---

1. Examples of non-conscious mental properties include beliefs that most of the time are not conscious, or our attitudes, drives, and motivations

SUBSTANCES AND PROPERTIES

The notion of a substance has a long history going back to Ancient Greek metaphysics, most prominently to Aristotle, and it has been understood in various ways since then. For present purposes we can say that a substance can be understood as a unified fundamental kind of entity—e.g. a person, or an animal—that can be the bearer of properties. In fact, the etymology of the Latin word *substantia* is that which lies below, that which exists underneath something else. So, for instance, a zebra can be a substance, which has properties, like a certain color, or a certain number of stripes. But the zebra is independent of its properties; it will continue to exist even if the properties were to change (and, according to some views, even if they ceased to exist altogether).

According to Cartesian dualism there are two kinds of substance: the material substance, which is extended in space and is divisible, and mental substances whose characteristic is thought. So each person is made up of these two substances—matter and mind—that are entirely different in kind and can exist independently of each other. Talking of the mind in terms of substances gives rise to a number of problems (see Chapter 1). To avoid these problems, property dualism argues that mentality should be understood in terms of properties, rather than substances: instead of saying that there are certain kinds of things that are minds, we say that to have a mind is to have certain properties. Properties are characteristics of things; properties are attributed to, and possessed by, substances. So according to property dualism there are different kinds of properties that pertain to the only kind of substance, the material substance: there are physical properties like having a certain color or shape, and there are mental properties like having certain beliefs, desires and perceptions.

Property dualism is contrasted with substance dualism since it posits only one kind of substance, but it is also contrasted with ontological monist views, such as materialism or idealism, according to which everything that exists (including properties) is of one kind. Usually, property dualism is put forward as an alternative to reductive physicalism (the type identity theory) – the view that all properties in the world can, in principle at least, be reduced to, or identified with, physical properties (Chapter 2).

Hilary Putnam's (1926-2016) multiple realization argument is a main reason why reductive physicalism is rejected by some philosophers, and it provides an argument for property dualism. Although this argument was originally used as an argument for functionalism, since it challenges the identity of mental states with physical states, it was taken up by non-reductive physicalists and property dualists alike. According to the multiple realization argument then, it is implausible to identify a certain kind of mental state, like pain, with a certain type of physical state since mental states might be implemented ("realized") in creatures (or even non-biological systems) that have a very different physical make up than our own. For instance, an octopus or an alien may very well feel pain but pain might be realized differently in their brains than it is in ours. So it seems that mental states can be "multiply realizable." This is incompatible with the idea that pain is strictly identical with one physical property, as the identity theory seems to claim. If this is correct, and there is no possibility of reduction of types of mental states to types of physical states, then mental properties and physical properties are distinct, which means that there are two different kinds of properties in the world and, therefore, property dualism is true.

In addition to the multiple realization argument, probably the most famous argument for property dualism is the knowledge argument put forward by Frank Jackson (1982). This argument involves the imaginary example of Mary, a brilliant neuroscientist who was raised in a black and white room. She knows everything there is to know about the physical facts about vision but she has never seen red (or any color for that matter). One day Mary leaves the black and white room sees a red tomato. Jackson claims that Mary learns something new upon seeing the red tomato—she learns what red looks like. Therefore, there must be more to learn about the world than just physical facts, and there are more properties in the world than just physical properties.

KINDS OF PROPERTY DUALISM

Property dualism can be divided into two kinds. The first kind of property dualism says that there are two kinds of properties, mental and physical, but mental properties are dependent on physical properties. This dependence is usually described in terms of the relation of supervenience. The basic idea of supervenience is that a property, A, supervenes on another property, B, if there cannot be a difference in A without a difference in B (though there can be differences in B with no change in A, which allows for the multiple realizability of mental properties). So, for example, if the aesthetic properties of a work of art supervene on its physical properties, there cannot be a change in its aesthetic properties unless there is a change in its physical properties. Or, if I feel fine now but have a headache five minutes from now, there must be a physical difference in my brain in these two moments. Another way of putting the idea that mental properties depend on physical properties is to say that if you duplicate all the physical properties of the world, you will automatically duplicate the mental properties as well—they would come "for free."

This kind of view is sometimes called non-reductive physicalism, and is often considered to be a form of property dualism, since it holds that there are two kinds of properties. Jaegwon Kim is a prominent supporter of the [irreducibility] of phenomenal properties (though he resists the term "property dualism" and prefers to call his position "something near enough" physicalism [2005]). Kim holds that intentional properties, like having a belief or hoping for something to happen, can be functionally reduced to physical properties.[2] However, this is not so for phenomenal properties (like tasting a particular taste or experiencing a certain kind of afterimage), which supervene on physical properties but cannot be reduced, functionally or otherwise, to physical properties.

According to Kim, there is a difference between intentional and phenomenal properties: Phenomenal (qualitative) mental states cannot be defined functionally, as intentional states can (or can in principle), and therefore cannot be reduced either. Briefly, the reason is that although phenomenal states can be associated with causal tasks these descriptions do not define or constitute pain. That is, though, pain can be associated with the state that is caused by tissue damage, that induces the belief that something is wrong with one's body and that results in pain-avoidance behavior, this is not what pain is. Pain is what it feels like to be in pain, it is a subjective feeling. In contrast, intentional states like beliefs and intentions are anchored to observable behaviour, and this feature makes them amenable

---

2. In functional reduction we identify the functional/causal role that the phenomenon we are interested plays and then reduce that role to a physical (token) state that realizes it. To use an example given by Kim in *Physicalism, Or Something Near Enough*, a gene is defined functionally as the mechanism that encodes and transmits genetic information. That is what a gene does. What "realizes" the role of the gene, however, are DNA molecules; genes are functionally reduced to DNA molecules. So a functional reduction identifies a functional/causal role with a physical state that realizes it (makes it happen, so to speak) and offers an explanation of how the physical state realizes the functional state.

to functional analysis. For instance, if a population of creatures interacts with its environment in a similar fashion to us (if those creatures interact with one another as we do, produce similar utterances and so forth), then we would naturally ascribe to these creatures beliefs, desires, and other intentional states, precisely because intentional properties are functional properties.

The second kind of property dualism, which is dualism in a more demanding sense, claims that there are two kinds of properties, physical and mental, and that mental properties are something over and above physical properties. This in turn can be understood in at least two ways. First, being "over and above" can mean that mental properties have independent causal powers, and are responsible for effects in the physical world. This is known as "downward causation." In this sense, a property dualist of this kind must believe that, say, the mental property of having the desire to get a drink is what actually causes you to get up and walk to the fridge, in contrast to some material property of your brain being the cause, like the firing of certain groups of neurons. Second, being something "over and above" must imply the denial of supervenience. In other words, for mental properties to be genuinely independent of physical properties, they must be able to vary independently of their physical bases. So a property dualist who denies supervenience would be committed to the possibility that two people can be in different mental states, e.g., one might be in pain and the other not, while having the same brain states.

Emergentism is a property dualist view in this more demanding sense. Emergentism first appeared as a systematic theory in the second half of the nineteenth century and the beginning of the twentieth century in the work of the so-called "British Emergentists," J.S.Mill (1806 –1873), Samuel Alexander (1859 –1938), C. Lloyd Morgan (1852 –1936) and C.D. Broad (1887 –1971). Since then it has been defended (and opposed) by many philosophers and scientists, some of whom understand it in different ways. Still, we can summarize the position by saying that according to emergentism, when a system reaches a certain level of complexity, entirely new properties emerge that are novel, irreducible to, and something "over and above" the lower level from which they emerged (Vintiadis 2013). For example, when a brain, or a nervous system, becomes complex enough new mental properties, like sensations, thoughts and desires, emerge from it in addition to its physical properties. So according to emergentism everything that exists is made up of matter but matter can have different kinds of properties, mental and physical, that are genuinely distinct in one or both of the senses described above: that is, either in the sense that mental properties have novel causal powers that are not to be found in physical properties underlying them or in the sense that mental properties do not supervene on physical properties.

Some philosophers have argued for the kind of demanding property dualism that denies supervenience by appealing to the conceivability of philosophical zombies—an argument most famously developed by David Chalmers. Philosophical zombies are beings that are behaviorally and physically just like us but that have no "inner" experience. If such beings are not only conceivable but also possible (as Chalmers argues), then it seems that there can be mental differences without physical differences (1996). If this argument is correct, then phenomenal properties cannot be explained in terms of physical properties and they are really distinct from physical properties.

OBJECTIONS TO PROPERTY DUALISM

A main problem for substance dualism was the question of mental causation. Given the view that the mental and the material substance are two discrete kinds of substances the problem that arises is that of their interaction, a problem posed by Princess Elizabeth of Bohemia (1618-1680) in her correspondence with Descartes. How can two different kinds of things have an effect on one another? It seems from what we know from science that physical effects have physical causes. If this is indeed the case, how is it that I can think of my grandmother and cry, or desire a glass of wine and go over to the fridge to pour myself one? How *do* the mental and the physical interact? The common consensus that substance dualism cannot satisfactorily answer this problem ultimately led many philosophers to the rejection of Cartesian dualism.

In the attempt to preserve the mental while also preserving a foothold in the physical, dualism of properties was introduced. However, the double requirement of the distinctness of physical properties from mental properties and of the dependence of mental properties on physical properties turns out to be a source of problems for property dualism as well.

This can be seen in the problem of causal exclusion that is analyzed below. This problem arises for property dualism and has been put forward by a number of philosophers over the years, most notably by Kim himself who, due to this problem, concludes that phenomenal properties that are irreducibly mental are also merely epiphenomenal, that is, they have no causal effects on physical events (2005).

According to mind-body supervenience, every time a mental property M is instantiated it supervenes on a physical property P.

$$M$$
$$\Uparrow$$
$$P$$

Now suppose M appears to cause another mental property M^1,

$$M \quad \rightarrow \quad M^1$$
$$\Uparrow$$
$$P$$

the question arises whether the cause of M^1 is indeed M or whether it is M^1's subjacent base P^1 (since according to supervenience M^1 is instantiated by a physical property P^1).

$$M \quad \rightarrow \quad M^1$$
$$\Uparrow \qquad\qquad \Uparrow$$
$$P \qquad\quad P^1$$

At this point we need to introduce two principles held by physicalists: First, the principle of causal closure according to which the physical world is causally closed. This means that every physical effect has a sufficient physical cause that brings it about. Note that this in itself does not exclude non-physical causes since such causes could also be part of the causal history of an effect. What does exclude such non-physical causes is a second principle which denies the overdetermination of events. According to this principle an effect cannot have more than one wholly sufficient cause (it cannot be overdetermined) and so this, along with causal closure, leads to the conclusion that when you trace the causes of an effect, all there are are physical causes.

To return to our example, given the denial of causal overdetermination, either M or P^1 is the cause of M^1—it can't be both—and so, given the supervenience relation, it seems that M^1 occurs because P^1 occurred. Therefore, it seems that M actually causes M^1 by causing the subjacent P^1 (and also that mental to mental, or same level, causation presupposes mental to physical, or downward, causation).

$$M \rightarrow M^1 \qquad\qquad M \rightarrow M^1$$
$$\Uparrow \qquad\qquad\qquad \Uparrow \searrow \Uparrow$$
$$P \qquad\qquad\qquad\quad P \qquad P^1$$

However, given the principle of causal closure P^1 must have a sufficient physical cause P.

$$M \qquad\quad M^1$$
$$\Uparrow \qquad\qquad \Uparrow$$
$$P \rightarrow P^1$$

But given exclusion again, P^1 cannot have two sufficient causes, M and P, and so P is the real cause of P^1 because if M were the real cause, causal closure would be violated again.

So the problem of causal exclusion is that, given supervenience, causal closure and the denial of overdetermination, it is not clear how mental properties can be causally efficacious; mental properties seem to be epiphenomenal, at best. And while epiphenomenalism is compatible with property dualism (since property dualism states that there are two kinds of properties in the world, and epiphenomenalism states that some mental properties are causally inert by-products of physical properties, thus accepting the existence of two properties), its coherence comes at the expense of our common sense intuitions that our mental states affect our physical states and our behavior. It seems then, that, for its critics, as far as mental causation goes, property dualism does not fare much better than substance dualism.

More generally, the question of the causal efficacy of mental properties gives rise to the same kinds of objections that were raised regarding mental causation in substance dualism. For instance, in both cases mental to physical interaction seems to violate the principle of conservation of energy, a principle that is considered to be fundamental to our physical science. That is, the conservation law would be violated if mental to physical causation were possible, since such an interaction would have to introduce energy to the physical world (assuming, that is, that the physical world is causally closed).

It is not in the scope of this discussion to wade into this matter, but it should be noted that this objection is not accepted by everyone; it has been argued that the principle of conservation of energy does not apply universally, for instance by citing examples from general relativity or quantum gravity. Similarly, both the causal closure of the physical and the denial of causal overdetermination have been questioned. Nonetheless, despite these responses, it is fair to say that the question of mental causation still remains one of the major objections to property dualism.

Another objection, this time to some views that are considered property dualist views, can be posed by asking, "In what way is property dualism really dualism?" In our distinction between two kinds of property dualism above, there is a clear sense in which positions of the second kind, like emergentism or views that deny supervenience, are property dualist positions. Since, for such views, mental properties are "something over and above" physical properties; they are distinct from them, irreducible to them and not wholly determined by them. So here we have cases of two genuinely different kinds of properties, and genuine cases of property dualism.

However, it is not equally clear that non-reductive physicalism can properly be called a kind of property dualism. The problem is that if mental properties are not something over and above physical properties then it is hard to see this as a genuine version of property dualism. We can see this if we look more closely into the meaning of physicalism.

Physicalism is the view that what there fundamentally is is what is described by physics. In this sense, mental properties are non-physical properties, since they are not properties to be found in physics. But if non-reductive physicalism claims that there are non-physical properties that are irreducible to physical properties, why should this be considered a case of physicalism? The answer given by the non-reductive physicalist is that this is because such properties are grounded in the physical realm through the relation of supervenience and that, although mental properties might not be identical to physical properties, they need to be at least in principle *explainable* in terms of physical properties (Horgan 1993). Indeed, non-reductive physicalism is sometimes called token identity theory because it claims that tokens (instances) of mental states can be identified with tokens of physical states, even if types of mental states are not identical with types of physical states. (An analogy: all instances of the property of being beautiful are physical—all beautiful objects are physical objects—but the property of being beautiful is not a physical property). But now the problem is that, as Tim Crane has argued, if physicalism requires that non-physical properties are explicable (even in principle) in physical terms it is not obvious why this position is a property dualist one, since for there to be genuine property dualism, the ontology of physics should not be enough to explain mental properties (2001). So, according to this objection, it seems that the mere denial of the identity of mental and physical properties is not enough for real property dualism, and also that real property dualists must either believe in downward causation or deny supervenience or both.

To sum up the above discussion, we can say that property dualism is a position that attempts to preserve the reality of mental properties while also giving them a foothold in the physical world. The need for this is evident, given the intractable difficulties presented by substance dualism on the one hand, and the problems faced by the identity theory on the other. However, despite the fact that property dualism enjoys renewed popularity these days, it is open to important objections that, for its critics, have not been adequately addressed and which render the position problematic.

REFERENCES

Chalmers, David J. 1996. *The Conscious Mind: In Search of a Fundamental Theory.* Oxford: Oxford University Press.

Crane, Tim. 2001. *Elements of Mind.* Oxford: Oxford University Press.

Horgan, Terence. 1993. "From Supervenience to Superdupervenience: Meeting the Demands of a Material World." *Mind* 102(408): 555-586.

Jackson, Frank. 1982. "Epiphenomenal Qualia." *Philosophical Quarterly* 32: 127-36.

Kim, Jaegwon. 2005. *Physicalism, Or Something Near Enough.* Princeton, NJ: Princeton University Press.

Vintiadis, Elly. 2013. "Emergence." In *Internet Encyclopedia of Philosophy. http://www.iep.utm.edu/emergenc/*

FURTHER READING

Kim, Jaegwon. 1998. *Philosophy Of Mind.* Boulder, CO/Oxford: Westview Press.

Maslin, K. T. 2007. *An Introduction to the Philosophy of Mind.* Cambridge: Polity Press.

CHAPTER 5.

QUALIA AND RAW FEELS

HENRY SHEVLIN

INTRODUCTION: WHAT ARE QUALIA?

As I sit writing this sentence, I am enjoying a wealth of experiences. In front of me, the sky is full of the pink and blue hues of approaching sunset dashed with white clouds. Tropical birds chitter in high-pitched trills, while a pair of dogs utter guttural barks at each other. My skin alternately prickles with the last lingering heat of the day, interrupted by the pleasant coolness of an evening breeze.

The scene I have just described is full of experiences with distinctive qualities—colours, sounds, and physical sensations. These qualities of experience are known to philosophers of mind as qualia, an oddly obscure term for an aspect of our lives that could scarcely be more familiar to us. Every waking moment of our lives, we are experiencing various qualia associated with sights, sounds, or feelings. Sometimes, we deliberately seek out new qualia, as when we order an unfamiliar dish at a restaurant, eager to learn what it tastes like. On other occasions, we seek urgently to put an end to some quale (the singular of "qualia") or another; for example, when we take an aspirin to relieve the throbbing sensation of a headache.

Qualia have been the focus of intense interest in philosophy of mind and cognitive science for several decades. They possess several apparent features that make them both fascinating and hard to explain. All of these properties are controversial (see section 4 below), but they certainly seem to capture several of the intuitive features of qualia.

First, qualia seem to be *private*: my qualia are a feature of my experience alone, and you can never directly access them. You may have wondered in the past whether other people experience colours in just the same way you do, or whether my blue may be your green. These questions arise precisely because of the apparent privacy of qualia. We can never know which qualia other people are experiencing.

Second (and related), qualia are arguably *ineffable*; that is, they cannot neatly be put into words. Imagine trying to explain to a person who is blind what red looks like, or (a less extreme example) conveying to a lifelong vegetarian what tuna tastes like. While in both cases, we might attempt to use metaphors ("red is like a trumpet") to convey the character of the experience, our attempts to do so will inevitably fail to do justice to the relevant sensation.

A final alleged property is that qualia are immediately and fully apprehensible to us just by experiencing them. In this respect, they are distinct from the *objects* of our experience. Imagine that you are lying in bed at night and hear a soft thud. You may well wonder what the noise was: a falling object, a door slamming in the wind, or perhaps your housemate returning home. What you don't have to speculate about, however, is what the noise *sounded* like to you. This is something you grasped simply by hearing it. More strongly and more controversially, some philosophers have suggested that we can never make errors of judgment about our qualia. If I say something feels painful to me, for example, then it is nonsensical to suggest I might be in error.

QUALIA AND THE MIND-BODY PROBLEM

One reason qualia have so fascinated philosophers is that they are arguably hard to explain in standard scientific terms. Many of us have probably heard neuroscientists talking about things like synapses, neurons, and different regions of the brain. It is perhaps not too difficult to see how this kind of scientific approach might explain various aspects of our behavior. We might understand perception, for example, in terms of the transmission of information from the sense organs through various processing areas of the brain, or unusual aggression in terms of the release of some hormone or neurotransmitter. It is much harder to see, however, how these kinds of scientific descriptions could ever give us a satisfying explanation of why red looks the specific way that it does, or why cinnamon tastes like *this* and vanilla like *that*.

The challenge here is not merely to explain the neuroscience of how vision works or how our tongue relates flavour information to the brain. Important progress is being made every day in understanding questions like these, although the science still has a long way to go. Instead, the real difficulty is that while science tells us about how the brain *works*, it seems unable to tell us what experiences are actually *like*. To get an idea of the problem, imagine a person who has been completely deaf since birth who wants to know what Beethoven sounds like. Even if we had perfect brain-scanners and could show them exactly what happens to someone's neurons when they listen to music, it does not seem like this could ever properly convey to them the subjective experience of hearing the opening bars of the Choral Symphony.

This creates an apparent challenge for a scientific worldview. If science cannot fully explain qualia, then does it follow that science can only offer us a partial understanding of the universe? More strongly, one might wonder whether the seeming inexplicability of qualia in scientific terms shows that the universe we inhabit does not consist solely of things like atoms, molecules, forces, and other objects from the domain of science, but also contains distinctive, irreducibly *mental* phenomena.

The challenge is well illustrated by a famous thought experiment called "Mary's Room" developed by philosopher Frank Jackson (1982).[1] Imagine a woman called Mary who is a brilliant scientist. Specifically, we are told that she knows all the physical facts about color perception: she knows all about the physics of light, the biology of the eye, and the neuroscience of color processing in the brain. However, Mary has never seen color herself, having spent her life in a black and white room. One day,

. Mary's Room is also discussed in Chapter 4.

Mary leaves her room, and sees a shiny red apple for the first time. "Wow!" she thinks, "So *that's* what red looks like."

Mary's Room attempts to demonstrate that there are certain facts that can't be accessed by scientific knowledge alone. After all, Mary *already* knows all the scientific facts about color before she leaves her room. What she lacks, however, is knowledge of the qualia of color; that is, what colors actually *look* like. She only gains this knowledge when she leaves the room and actually sees colors herself. Hence, the argument runs, there are certain facts that cannot be explained by science, but instead rely on subjective experience. The argument can be presented formally as follows.

1. Mary knows all the scientific facts about color before she leaves her room.

2. Mary learns new facts (about what colors look like) when she leaves her room.

3. Therefore, not all facts are scientific facts.

Mary's Room is one of the most famous thought experiments in all of philosophy and has generated a vast number of responses. Most of them challenge premise (2), above, and argue that in fact Mary doesn't learn anything new when she leaves her room.

For example, the ability hypothesis claims that what Mary gains is not knowledge but a new set of abilities (Lewis 1990). Imagine someone who knows a lot about music, but can't play any instruments. However, after lots of practice, they learn to play the piano. The ability hypothesis suggests that something like this applies to Mary. Prior to leaving her room, she had never seen red objects, so couldn't recognize a given object as red, or imagine or remember the color red. After leaving the room, her new experiences of red allow her to do all of this. Our sense that she gains knowledge, then, is misplaced—what she gains is a new kind of skill. Some philosophers doubt that this adequately explains away our sense that Mary really does gain a new special kind of knowledge when she leaves her black and white room.

Another important approach we can term the old fact, new knowledge view.[2] Imagine someone knows that Istanbul was founded in 330AD. They then learn quite separately that Constantinople was founded in 330AD. Assuming they do not already know that Istanbul and Constantinople are the same city, it seems reasonable to say that the person learned something new when they heard the information about Constantinople. Certainly, they have an item of trivia at their disposal that they didn't have before. However, since "Constantinople" in fact refers to the same city as "Istanbul," we should also say that they have not strictly learned any *new* fact about the universe, having instead encountered a fact she already knew in a different form. Applied to the Mary case, the idea is that Mary really *did* know all facts about color before she left her room. When she sees red for the first time, she simply encounters these same facts in a new way, namely via her own color vision rather

2. See, e.g., Michael Tye, *Ten Problems of Consciousness*, 171-77 (Cambridge, MA: MIT Press, 1995).

than via the theoretical language of science. One challenge for this view is to offer a developed account of this special experiential way of gaining knowledge while avoiding appeal to any non-scientific or non-physical facts or properties.

A final approach adopted by some defiant philosophers is to insist that Mary would not gain *any* kind of new knowledge or ability toward the world when she leaves her room. If she *really* knew all the scientific facts about color before leaving the room, she would in fact already have all the knowledge and abilities associated with seeing colors, despite never having personally seen them (Dennett 2006). This might sound like a flat denial of the powerful intuition motivating the thought experiment. One way to make this approach more persuasive, however, is to focus on the first premise of the argument above, that Mary knows *all* relevant the scientific facts. Is this really something we can easily imagine? After all, current science is still incomplete, and falls far short of providing us with knowledge of every fact even within its own domain of explanation. Moreover, most scientists are so specialized they know only a small proportion of the facts within their own field. Mary, then, would have be more like a superintelligence from the distant future than a normal human. Given this, should our intuitions about what we can imagine be given much weight?

These responses are only a fraction of the many approaches to Mary's Room adopted by philosophers. While considerable progress has been made in developing rebuttals to Mary's Room, it is probably fair to say that there is no one response that has been generally accepted as solving the problem. The puzzle of qualia for the scientific worldview, then, remains a central area of philosophical research.

HOW MANY KINDS OF QUALIA ARE THERE?

A further important debate about qualia concerns which kinds of mental states actually have them. The usual examples of qualia are things like sights, sounds, and bodily sensations. But some philosophers have argued that there are plenty of other kinds of qualia besides these.

Some example candidates for these additional qualia are things like emotions. It certainly seems like there is a distinctive feeling (or set of feelings) associated with powerful emotions like joy, anger, or sadness, for example. However, it remains controversial whether these feelings involve a special kind of qualia all of their own, or might be understood instead in terms of other qualia, such as, for example, those associated with bodily sensations, a view adopted by one of the founders of modern psychology, William James (1842-1910), in a famous article (1884). Note, for example, the intense physical sensations that accompany the emotion of excitement: we may experience the feeling of our heart rate going up, our mouth becoming dry, and our muscles tensing. Could such "bodily qualia" be all there is to the qualia of emotions? The issue remains hotly debated.

Another important debate concerns the range or type of qualia associated with perception. We can all agree that there are qualia associated with our experiences of color and shape, for example. But could there be special kinds of qualia involved in seeing someone as looking friendly, for example, or in recognizing an animal as a raccoon? The idea that there are such "high-level" qualia associated with properties beyond things like color, shape, and motion is sometimes called the rich content view (Siegel 2010). One way to motivate this idea comes from cases where the character of our experience—in other words, our qualia—seems to change despite there being no changes in how we are experiencing the lower level qualities of color, shape, and so on.

Consider, for example, the famous "duck-rabbit" illusion below (Jastrow 1899). With a little mental effort, we can "switch" from seeing the picture as a duck to seeing it as a rabbit, and it arguably seems like there is a shift in the way the picture looks. However, it is far from clear that our experience of the low-level features of the image—the colors and shapes—actually changes. If that is right, then it might provide evidence that there are special kinds of qualia associated with seeing the image *as a duck* and seeing it *as a rabbit*.

A final important debate concerns whether non-perceptual states like thinking and understanding might have special qualia associated with them. For example, quickly add together the numbers 17 and 48 in your head, and in doing so, consider what feelings or qualities are associated with the experience. Was there a distinctive kind of feeling that accompanied your thoughts about the numbers? Some philosophers have suggested that there is indeed a kind of special experience associated with thinking and understanding.[3] One argument for this kind of "cognitive qualia" (or cognitive phenomenology, as it is also known) comes from cases of hearing a foreign language. Imagine that Jack, an English speaker, and Jacques, a French speaker, are both listening to a French radio broadcast. Jack cannot understand what he is hearing, but Jacques can. Intuitively, it seems like there is a difference in the quality of their two experiences arising from the differences in their understanding (or lack thereof). Again, the existence of these cognitive qualia is hotly contested. Some philosophers claim, for example, that the qualities associated with experiences like thinking and understanding can be understood just in terms of regular perceptual qualia, like colors and shapes, occurring as images in our minds. Hence, perhaps any qualia you experienced in thinking through the math problem above were just a matter of seeing or hearing the numbers in your "mind's eye."

SKEPTICISM ABOUT QUALIA

We have been talking in this chapter about qualia as though their existence, at least, was uncontroversial. In one sense, that is surely true: no one could deny that we genuinely experience

3. See Galen Strawson, *Mental Reality* (MIT Press, 1994), Ch.1.

colors and tastes, for example. Some philosophers remain skeptical about qualia, however, insisting that the very idea is a confused one. The philosopher Daniel Dennett is one such famous skeptic. In a classic paper, "Quining Qualia," he gives a number of examples of cases in which the idea of qualia as used by philosophers seems to invite impossible and perhaps nonsensical questions (1988). Consider, for example, the case of two people, one of whom loves cauliflower, and the other of whom despises it. Should we say in such an instance that they must therefore have different qualia when they taste cauliflower, or instead say that they have different reactions to the same qualia? Dennett would have us believe that such questions barely make sense.

To illustrate the point further, he invites us to imagine that we ourselves go from despising cauliflower to loving it (an experience many of us have had with one food item or another). Even in such a case, he suggests, we are not able to say whether our qualia have changed or our attitudes have changed. If that is right, then it seems that some questions about qualia cannot be answered from the first-person perspective; but given that qualia are supposedly private and ineffable, it would seem to follow that they cannot be answered at all! Rather than embrace such mysterious entities, Dennett suggests, we would do better to abandon the very idea of qualia as confused.

Another kind of skepticism about qualia concerns their relationship to the objects of our experience. For a long time, many philosophers thought of qualia as things we could observe in our experience in their own right, quite separate from our experience of objects in the world (hence the term "raw feels" sometimes used to describe them). Other philosophers have more recently challenged this idea, instead claiming that insofar as we experience qualia at all, we experience them as properties of objects in the world (Harman 1990). This is a complex debate, but in essence, these philosophers claim that in looking at a green tree, we do not experience "raw greenness." Rather, what we might call the "qualia of greenness" are actually experienced as properties of an object in the world, namely the tree itself. If this transparency thesis is correct, then it suggests that even if qualia exist, they might simply be an aspect of our awareness of real objects in the world, rather than some mysterious "mental paint" (Block 1996). If so, cognitive science might enable us to understand qualia via the broader philosophical and scientific project of explaining how perception makes us aware of the world.

CONCLUSION

Qualia remain one of the deepest puzzles in all of philosophy, and this chapter has only offered a cursory survey of some of the most important debates in which they feature. Even while science has given us tremendous new insights into difficult questions like the origins of the universe and the human genome, the problem of how to explain qualia seems still tantalizingly out of reach of standard scientific enquiry. Despite or perhaps because of this, many philosophers and scientists view qualia as a vital and exciting frontier for human understanding.

REFERENCES

Block, Ned. 1996. "Mental Paint and Mental Latex." *Philosophical Issues* 7(19).

Dennett, Daniel C. 2006. "What Robomary Knows." In *Phenomenal Concepts and Phenomenal Knowledge: New Essays on Consciousness and Physicalism*, ed. Torin Alter and SvenWalter. Oxford: Oxford University Press.

Dennett, Daniel C. 1988. "Quining Qualia." In *Consciousness in Contemporary Science*, 42-77. New York: Clarendon Press/Oxford University Press.

Harman, Gilbert. 1990. "The Intrinsic Quality of Experience." *Philosophical Perspectives* 4: 31-52.

Jackson, Frank. 1982. "Epiphenomenal Qualia." *Philosophical Quarterly* 32: 127-36.

Lewis, David. 1990. "What Experience Teaches." In *Mind and Cognition*, ed. William G. Lycan, 29-57. Oxford: Basil Blackwell.

James, William. 1884. "What Is an Emotion?" *Mind* 9(34): 188-205.

Jastrow, Joseph. 1899. The Mind's Eye. *Popular Science Monthly* 54: 299-312.

Siegel, Susanna. 2010. *The Contents of Visual Experience.* Oxford: Oxford University Press.

FURTHER READING

Alter, Torin and Robert J. Howell. 2009. *A Dialogue on Consciousness.* Oxford: Oxford University Press.

Blackmore, Susan. 2006. *Conversations on Consciousness.* New York/Oxford: Oxford University Press.

Chalmers, David J. 1998. *The Conscious Mind: In Search of a Fundamental Theory.* New York/Oxford: Oxford University Press.

Dennett, Daniel C. 1991. *Consciousness Explained.* United States: Little, Brown and Co.

Montero, Barbara. 1999. "The Body Problem." *Noûs* 33(2): 183-200.

Nagel, Thomas. 1974. "What is it Like to be a Bat?" *Philosophical Review* 83: 435-456.

Media Attributions

- Duck-Rabbit Illusion (or Optical illusion of a duck or a rabbit head) by Anonymous Illustrator © Public Domain

CHAPTER 6.

CONSCIOUSNESS

TONY CHENG

INTRODUCTION

The term "consciousness" is very often, though not always, interchangeable with the term "awareness," which is more colloquial to many ears. We say things like "are you aware that …" often. Sometimes we say "have you noticed that … ?" to express similar thoughts, and this indicates a close connection between consciousness (awareness) and attention (noticing), which we will come back to later in this chapter. Ned Block, one of the key figures in this area, provides a useful characterization of what he calls "phenomenal consciousness." For him, phenomenal consciousness is experience. Experience covers perceptions, e.g., when we see, hear, touch, smell, and taste, we typically have experiences, such as seeing colors and smelling odors. It also covers bodily awareness, e.g., we typically have experiences of our own bodily temperature and positions of limbs. Consciousness is primarily about this experiential aspect of our mental lives.

Most discussions of philosophy of mind rely on the idea of conscious experience on some level. Descartes reported his conscious experiences in his *Meditations on First Philosophy.* These figured centrally into his arguments that he has a mind (Chapter 1). Behaviorism, materialism, functionalism, and property dualism seek to explain our mental lives, so they will need to include consciousness, as it is one of the most important elements of mentality (Chapter 2, Chapter 3, Chapter 4). Qualia and raw feels are one way to understand consciousness; since they have been covered earlier (Chapter 5), we will not discuss them here. Knowledge, belief, and other mental states are sometimes, though not always conscious, so it is important to understand the difference between (say) conscious and unconscious beliefs. This also applies to concepts and content (Chapter 7). Whether freedom of the will and the self require consciousness is highly debated (Chapter 8). In this way, it can be seen that consciousness has a central place in philosophy of mind.

CONCEPTS OF CONSCIOUSNESS

There are many concepts of consciousness; in general there are two approaches. First, one can survey folk concepts of consciousness: how lay people use the term, and how they use other related terms (e.g., awareness) to refer to similar phenomena. Second, one can search for useful concepts of consciousness for explaining or understanding the mind. The former approach is conducted in experimental philosophy, a relatively new branch of philosophy, which invokes experimental methods to survey people's concepts, including those who are from diverse cultural and linguistic backgrounds. In this chapter, we will rather focus on the latter approach, which is traditionally favored by philosophers of mind.

Philosophers have different ways of picking out various concepts of consciousness, and they tend to strongly disagree with one another. No division is entirely uncontroversial. However, there is one distinction that tends to be the starting point of philosophical discussions about consciousness; even those who disagree with this way of carving out of the territory often start from here. It is the distinction from Block (1995) on phenomenal and access consciousness:

> Phenomenal consciousness [P-consciousness] is experience; what makes a state phenomenally conscious is that there is something "it is like" (Nagel 1974) to be in that state. (Block 1995, 228)

> A perceptual state is access-conscious [A-conscious], roughly speaking, if its content—what is represented by the perceptual state—is processed via that information-processing function, that is, if its content gets to the Executive System, whereby it can be used to control reasoning and behavior. (1995, 229)[1]

Block also discusses a third concept of consciousness, called "monitoring consciousness" (1995, 235).[2] In order to be focused, we will restrict ourselves to the division between phenomenal and access consciousness.

Block's main point is to dissociate P-consciousness and A-consciousness: he seeks to make the case that these two kinds of consciousness are different in kind. In order to do so, he first tries to find cases in which P-consciousness exists while A-consciousness is absent:

> [S]uppose you are engaged in intense conversation when suddenly at noon you realize that right outside your window there is—and has always been for sometime—a deafening pneumatic drill digging up the street. You were aware of the noise all along, but only at noon are you *consciously* aware of it. That is, you were P-conscious of the noise all along, but at noon you are both P-conscious *and* A-conscious of it. (1995, 234; original emphasis)

For A-consciousness without P-consciousness, Block argues that it is hard to find any actual case, but it is "conceptually possible" (1995, 233), meaning that there is no incoherence in the scenario in which A-consciousness exists while P-consciousness is absent. This strategy is effective since what he wants to argue is that these two kinds of consciousness are distinct: for this purpose, there is no need to have actual cases in which one exists while the other is absent, though actual cases do help as they serve as existential proofs.

Another distinction that needs to be in place is from David Chalmers (1995). He poses a challenge to researchers of consciousness with the distinction between the "easy problems" and the "hard problems" of consciousness. According to Chalmers,

> [t]he easy problems of consciousness are those that seem directly susceptible to the standard methods of cognitive science, whereby a phenomenon is explained in terms of computational or neural mechanisms. The hard problems are those that seem to resist those methods. (1995, 4)

1. For more on representation and content, see Chapter 7.
2. For more concepts of consciousness, see Tye (2003).

Here are some examples of the easy problems he provides:

The integration of information by a cognitive system;

The reportability of mental states;

The ability of a system to access its own internal states;

The focus of attention (1995).

Both the easy problems and the hard problems interest philosophers. Block's discussion of P- and A-consciousness can be seen as primarily in the territory of easy problems, while Chapters 1 to 5 of this book can be seen as more about the hard problems.

Now, with these two basic distinctions at hand, it is time to see how philosophers and scientists theorize about different kinds of consciousness, especially phenomenal consciousness.

THEORIES OF CONSCIOUSNESS

Block seeks to dissociate P- and A-consciousness. He has several argumentative lines; the most relevant one has it that P-consciousness cannot be explained by representational contents. To understand what this amounts to, one needs to have some basic grip on what representational contents are. Again, examples will help. Two beliefs are different because they have different contents: my belief that tomorrow will rain and that the day after tomorrow will not rain are different beliefs because their contents—"tomorrow will rain" and "the day after tomorrow will not rain"—are different. These contents are said to represent states of affairs, including actual ones and imaginary ones. Contents can be true or false: my belief that tomorrow it will rain can fail to be true simply because tomorrow it will not rain. Representational content itself is a complex topic that cannot be handled in this chapter; it will be the subject matter of Chapter 7. There can be many reasons for believing that P-consciousness cannot be explained by representational contents, one being that an experience and a belief can share the same content, but have different phenomenology. This is debatable. Some would argue that experiences do not have representational content.[3]

Now, content and consciousness are two major topics in philosophy of mind. Another main figure in this area, Daniel Dennett, has them as his first book's title (1969). They are often studied separately, but some philosophers have attempted to invoke one to explain the other. The most prominent position, exemplified by Fred Dretske (1995), holds that representational content is relatively easier to understand, since it can be explained by naturalistic notions such as information; it is naturalistic in the sense that natural sciences would find those notions scientifically respectable. This view further holds that consciousness should be understood through representational content, so that it is fully naturalized. This view is representationalism. The canonical statement of it is that "all mental facts are representational facts" (Dretske 1995, xiii). This is the "naturalizing the mind" project. Now, although Block is all for the naturalization project, he objects to this specific way of naturalizing consciousness. The basic intuition is that representationalism leaves something crucial out: the *what-it-is-like*-ness of experience. This is because, for example, beliefs with representational contents can be unconscious. Or again: some hold that experiences do not have content.

See Travis (2004), for example.

Although Block and others have been resisting representationalism, it is still the most prominent view in this area. This is presumably because it offers the most promising line of naturalizing the mind according to many. This is important as one of the main motives in twentieth-century philosophy is to situate the mind in the physical world (more on this in Chapters 1-5). Now, this prominent theory comes in various forms, which each of the following sections will summarize.

First-Order Representationalism

This is the view that representational content can exclusively explain phenomenal consciousness (Dretske 1995, Tye 1995). It is either argued that they are identical, or the latter supervenes on the former. Supervenience is another technical concept that can be seen in many areas in philosophy. Suppose A is the supervenience base, and B is said to supervene on A. In this case, if B has any change, it has to be because there is some change in A. But the other way around is not true: it can happen that B stays the same while A has changed. This is a specific way to explain the dependence relation. It would help to see this with a concrete example. In ethics, it has been argued that facts in ethics, e.g., torturing is wrong, have solid status because they supervene on facts in physics. In this case, if ethical facts have any change, it has to be because there are some changes in physical facts. But the other way around is not true: it can happen that ethical facts stay the same while physical facts have changed. The same move has been invoked in explaining aesthetic facts. This notion of supervenience seems to capture what we need for the dependence relation: physical facts are the most fundamental, so if other facts change, it has to be due to changes in physical facts. But different physical facts can sustain the same ethical, aesthetic, and mental facts. This is one powerful thought that is behind representationalism.

Higher-Order Representationalism

Higher-order theories in general hold that a state is conscious in virtue of being accompanied by other states. How to characterize the relevant sense of "accompany" is of course a difficult and controversial matter (Rosenthal 2005). One crucial motivation for higher-order theories is David Rosenthal's observation that "mental states are conscious only if one is in some way conscious of them" (2005, 4; my emphasis). He calls this the "transitivity principle." Notice that "only if" signifies a particular logical relation: "A only if B" means B is necessary for A. So this principle says that one's consciousness of some mental states is a necessary condition of those mental states being conscious.

Higher-order theories come in many varieties. The basic question is about the nature of the relevant higher-order states. They are either conceived as perception or thought. The former can be found in Armstrong (1968) and Lycan (1996), and it is also called the "inner sense theory." The idea is that just like ordinary perceptions (outer sense), the internal consciousness-making states are also perceptual (inner sense). What is crucial here is that perception is a lower level state comparing with thought. One merit of this version is that perception is more primitive than thoughts, so it can more easily accommodate the case of non-linguistic animals, since they can perceive but might not be able to think.

The latter—higher-order thought theories—has two versions. Rosenthal (2005) holds that phenomenally conscious mental states are the objects of higher-order thoughts. This is actualist

4. Also see Lycan (1996).

Carruthers (2005) holds that phenomenally conscious mental states are available to higher-order thoughts. This is dispositionalist. The distinction between actual and dispositional is also important in many areas in philosophy. Think about documents in your laptop. Since you have the relevant passwords, those documents are accessible or available to you, but it does not mean that at any specific moment you are accessing any specific document. Putting it bluntly, for the actualist, only those mental states that I am actually accessing at any given moment are conscious, while for the dispositionalist, any mental states that I could at some point access are conscious. In general, the dispositional accounts are less demanding than the actualist accounts, simply because dispositional notions are in general weaker. But all these higher-order theories can be classified as versions of representationalism, since both perceptions and thoughts have contents, according to most views.

Reflexive Representationalism

This view might be difficult differentiate from higher-order theories. The basic idea is that phenomenally conscious mental states themselves possess higher-order representational contents that represent the states themselves (Kriegel 2009). The main merit of this view is that it does not duplicate mental states: the contents are part of the relevant conscious states. For example, my visual experience of seeing the book in front of me has some specific conscious phenomenology, and also the content that there is a book in front of me. This view would say that this visual experience has the phenomenology it does due to the content it possesses. This group of ideas come in so many varieties that we cannot cover them here, but it is worth bearing in mind that this should not be conflated with higher-order theories.

It is controversial whether the next two groups should be classified as representationalism. This chapter doesn't take a stand with regard to this further question.

Cognitive Theories

This group of ideas invokes cognition to understand consciousness. In a way it is quite similar to standard representationalism, since contents are often attributed to cognitive states such as beliefs. However, they are crucially different in that cognitive theories typically do not invoke representational content, which is primarily a notion from philosophy. The most famous cognitive theory is proposed by scientist Bernard Baars (1988): according to this view, consciousness emerges from competitions among processors and outputs for a limited working memory capacity that broadcasts information for access in a "global workspace." One can think of the model with the analogy from digital computers. This is quite similar to Dennett's multiple drafts model, according to which different probes would elicit different answers about the subject's conscious states (1991). They are similar in the sense that both theories invoke cognitive notions to explain consciousness. Cognitive theories tend to be quite naturalistic, though they do not use representational contents to explain consciousness. Block argues against cognitive theories with similar reasons against representational views, i.e., they cannot capture the *what-it-is-like*-ness of experience.

Information Integration Theory

Most researchers agree that information must play some role in the complete theory of consciousness, but exactly what role it plays is controversial. Information Integration Theory, or IIT, is a view that assigns a very significant role to information proposed by neuroscientist Giulio Tononi (2008). He argues that the relevant kind of information integration is necessary and sufficient for consciousness. According to this view, consciousness is a purely information-theoretic property of cognitive systems, i.e., no other notion is more fundamental in this regard. The details of this theory are quite technical, and it needs to be further developed as it is quite young. Some have also compared it with panpsychism, the view that consciousness is one of the most fundamental properties of the world (Chalmers 1996). But we need to bear in mind that every theory is distinctive and needs to be understood in its own terms.

This ends our summary of some major theories of consciousness. It is not supposed to be comprehensive, and each theory discussed above has many more details that need to be taken seriously. This summary, and this chapter as a whole, serve only as a starting point for further exploration.

ATTENTION AND CONSCIOUSNESS

At the beginning of this chapter, we saw that there are potential connections between attention and consciousness. Typically, chapters on consciousness do not discuss attention. Since 2010 or so, however, philosophical discussions of attention have become more widespread, so it makes sense to discuss it in relation to consciousness, even if only briefly.

Before the 1990s, "consciousness" was a term that scientists tried to stay away from. It was regarded as unscientific, as there was no respectable way to give it a satisfactory operational definition, i.e., it was difficult to give a definition that was grounded in empirical evidence. Back then, scientists studied attention instead, as it was easier to quantify it, or so it seemed. Empirical studies of attention have been fruitful since the 1960s. Now, although scientists tried hard to avoid talking about consciousness explicitly, it was not possible to ignore it entirely. For example, when psychologist Max Coltheart defines "visible persistence" (1980), it is hard to understand what we should mean by "visible" if it is different from "consciously seen," though there can indeed be other interpretations, such as "able to be seen." But one wonders whether that should mean "able to be *consciously* seen." Of course there are subtleties here; for example Block (2007) further distinguishes between visible persistence and phenomenal persistence, which makes one wonder how to understand visible persistence exactly. But in any case, before the 1990s or so, attention was intensely studied by scientists, and in a way it served as a surrogate for consciousness, as attention is more scientifically respectable according to many.

The situation has dramatically changed. Nowadays consciousness studies are pervasive not only in sciences but also in philosophy. The reasons for this are complicated; it is not simply because nowadays consciousness can be better defined in sciences. (I shall not touch on this complex history here.) Now the question concerning the relation between attention and consciousness arises: Are they identical? If not, how do they relate to each other? It is hard to maintain that they are identical, as there seem to be clear cases in which a subject, not necessarily a human subject, can focus its attention while being unconscious of the target. Perhaps that subject is a simple organism that is not conscious in the relevant sense, but arguably it has certain basic attentional capacities, i.e., they can deploy their cognitive resources to focus on specific targets. Normally the question is more about whether attention is necessary and/or sufficient for consciousness. Jesse Prinz (2012) argues for this strong view, and sometimes he comes close to the identity view. This view faces two basic challenges: Some have argued that attention is not necessary for consciousness; the phenomenological overflow view held by Block (2007) is one such view. Some have argued that attention is not sufficient for consciousness; Robert Kentridge and colleagues (1999) have argued that the case of blindsight—patients who are blind in certain parts of their visual fields due to cortical damages—is attention without awareness, since these patients exemplify clear markers of attention, while the patients themselves also insist that they are unconscious of the relevant parts of the visual fields. Now, these are all highly debatable and there is much room to disagree (Cheng 2017). Both consciousness and attention are still heated topics nowadays, and will continue to be so in the foreseeable future.

REFERENCES

Armstrong, David. 1968. *A Materialist Theory of the Mind*. London: Routledge.

Baars, Bernard. 1988. *A Cognitive Theory of Consciousness*. Cambridge, UK: Cambridge University Press.

Block, Ned. 1995. "On a Confusion about a Function of Consciousness." *Behavioral and Brain Sciences* 18: 227-287.

Block, Ned. 2007. "Consciousness, Accessibility and the Mesh between Psychology and Neuroscience." *Behavioral and Brain Sciences* 30: 481-548.

Carruthers, Peter. 2005. *Consciousness: Essays from a Higher-Order Perspective*. Oxford: Oxford University Press.

Chalmers, David. 1995. "Facing up to the Problem of Consciousness." *Journal of Consciousness Studies* 2(3): 200-219.

Chalmers, David. 1996. *The Conscious Mind: In Search of a Fundamental Theory*. New York: Oxford University Press.

Cheng, Tony. 2017. "Iconic Memory and Attention in the Overflow Debate." *Cogent Psychology* 4.

Coltheart, Max. 1980. "Iconic Memory and Visible Persistence." *Perception and Psychophysics* 27(3): 183-228.

Dennett, Daniel. 1969. *Content and Consciousness*. Oxon: Routledge & Kegan Paul.

Dennett, Daniel. 1991. *Consciousness Explained*. New York: Little Brown & Co.

Dretske, Fred. 1995. *Naturalizing the Mind*. Cambridge, MA: MIT Press.

Kentridge, Robert et al. 1999. "Attention without Awareness in Blindsight." *Proceedings of the Royal Society of London* (B) 266: 1805-1811.

Kriegel, Uriah. 2009. *Subjective Consciousness: A Self-Representational Theory*. Oxford: Oxford University Press.

Lycan, William. 1996. *Consciousness and Experience*. Cambridge, MA: MIT Press.

Nagel, Thomas. 1974. "What is it like to be a Bat?" *Philosophical Review* 83: 435-450.

Prinz, Jesse. 2012. *The Consciousness Brain: How Attention Engenders Experience*. New York: Oxford University Press.

Rosenthal, David. 2005. *Consciousness and Mind*. Oxford: Oxford University Press.

Tononi, Giulio. 2008. "Consciousness as Integrated Information: A Provisional Manifesto." *Biological Bulletin* 215: 216-242.

Travis, Charles. 2004. "The Silence of the Senses." *Mind* 113: 57-94.

Tye, Michael. 1995. *Ten Problems of Consciousness: A Representational Theory of the Phenomenal Mind*. Cambridge, MA: MIT Press.

Tye, Michael. 2003. *Consciousness and Persons: Unity and Identity*. Cambridge, MA: MIT Press.

FURTHER READING

Blackmore, Susan and Emily Troscianko. 2018. *Consciousness: An Introduction*. Oxford: Routledge.

Churchland, Patricia. 1989. *Neurophilosopy: Toward a Unified Science of the Mind-Brain*. Cambridge, MA: MIT Press.

Hurley, Susan. 1998. *Consciousness in Action*. Cambridge, MA: MIT Press.

CHAPTER 7.

CONCEPTS AND CONTENT

ERAN ASOULIN

INTRODUCTION

The problem of intentionality is the problem of how some entities can be "about" something. That is, sentences, thoughts, or concepts, among others, display intentionality in that they are about something else; they are said to be a representation of something. The notion of intentionality can be traced back at least as far as Aristotle (384 BCE-322 BCE), though the German philosopher Franz Brentano (1838-1917) is generally credited with introducing the notion to contemporary philosophy in the late nineteenth century. Brentano's oft-quoted remark is that "Every mental phenomenon is characterized by ... the intentional (or mental) inexistence of an object" and "reference to a content, direction toward an object." In other words, "Every mental phenomenon includes something as object within itself, although they do not all do so in the same way. In presentation something is presented, in judgement something is affirmed or denied, in love loved, in hate hated, in desire desired and so on" (Brentano [1874] 1995, 68). The usual way to frame the problem of intentionality is in terms of the notion of meaning or content. What is the status of the meaning of a sentence over and above its formal and syntactic aspects? What makes it the case that a particular proposition has the content that it does? Is content only dependent upon mind-internal properties? Or must we make use of mind-external factors such as the context of the utterance or the speaker's social history in order to determine the content? Those who argue that the relevant and scientifically interesting properties that are involved in content are overwhelmingly, though not entirely, within the mind are referred to as internalists. On the other hand, externalists argue that there is something more to content than merely mind-internal events and their happenstance connection to the world: externalists insist that the meanings of our words (or sentences, or the contents of our thoughts, etc.) depend on some deep metaphysical (perhaps causal) connection between the mind and other worldly objects that are independent of the mind.

Externalists argue that a theory of content needs to provide an account of the relation between linguistic expressions and what may be called things in the world. In other words, the claim is that in order to explain content we must provide an account of the relation between linguistic expressions and the things that they can be used to talk about. Or as Colin McGinn puts it: "[E]xternalism supposes there to be a deep connection between states of mind and conditions in the nonmental world. Is the mind fundamentally autonomous with respect to the world, or does the world enter into the very nature of the mind?" (McGinn 1989, 1) He remarks further that according to externalism, "The environment is thus held to be constitutive of the very nature of mental states, determining what they are." McGinn argues that internalism "insists upon … drawing a sharp line between mind and world; but the externalist holds that the mind is penetrated by the world, configured by it" (1989, 3). That said, however, we will see that the main force and substance of the internalist position is not exactly a mirror image or a negation of the externalist position, for internalism only denies that there is a deep metaphysical relation between the things in the world and linguistic expressions. That is, internalists dispute the externalist claim that the relations between linguistic expressions and the things in the world are desirable or even tractable in an explanatory theory of content.

This chapter is structured as follows. First I discuss the nature of concepts. I then discuss externalism and the way in which it explains the nature of concepts and their content. I discuss one of the major thought experiments that have motivated many philosophers to adopt the externalist position. I then discuss the internalist position, which not only provides objections to the main claims of externalism but also provides its own positive account of concepts and their content.

WHAT IS A CONCEPT?

A concept is generally understood in the philosophy of mind to refer to a constituent of thought. Consider the proposition "John thinks that the book is on the table." Following Bertrand Russell (1872-1970), philosophers speak of propositional attitudes, which include beliefs, desires, hopes, fears, expectations, and any other attitude that involves a proposition. A propositional attitude of the form "X thinks that P" has two parts. The first constitutes the verb of the psychological-state description and contains information about the agent and the agent's psychological state. That is, the first part gives information about who takes which propositional attitude (for example, "John thinks"). The second part completes the description by revealing what the proposition is, or what the attitude refers to (for example, "that the book is on the table"). Concepts are said to be the constituents of the propositions expressed by propositional attitudes (in this case the concepts are, roughly, "book," "table," and "on"). Propositional attitudes and thus concepts are used in folk psychological (or intentional) explanations of behavior.

A simple example of the explanations and predictions that folk psychology allows is as follows. Suppose that we wish to explain why Leila chose to take her umbrella with her when she departed today. We can make use of some propositional attitudes and certain laws of folk psychology to formulate such an explanation. For instance, Leila believes that it will rain today (perhaps she heard the weather forecast on the radio), Leila believes that using an umbrella will help her seek shelter from rain, Leila desires not to get wet today. Therefore, since, all things being equal, humans act in accordance with their beliefs and desires, we can explain why Leila took her umbrella with her today. In other words, she took the umbrella because she believed X and desired Y, and believed that by doing Z she can bring it about that Y (notice that this is a counterfactual, so that if she did not believe that X and did not desire that Y then she would not do Z). Since beliefs and desires are integral parts of human thought, and since beliefs, say, are thought of as expressing propositions, the central role of concepts in philosophy and psychology is clear. That is, since the constituents of propositions are concepts, the need to explain the nature of concepts is inseparable from a theory of how the mind works.

Concepts are clearly shared between different people, and the question of what it is that is shared can be understood as the question of what the nature of content is. That is, if both John and Leila think that P, then they both share the content inherent in the concepts of the proposition P. What this claim amounts to is cashed out in very different ways by externalists and internalists, especially in terms of what explanatory role content is supposed to play. Externalists are mostly interested in concepts insofar as they figure in explanations of behavior (linguistic or other), whereas internalists are interested in concepts insofar as they serve as the meanings of linguistic items. Thus, a focus of internalist semantics is the underlying mechanisms of conceptual structure in virtue of which language production and comprehension is made possible. Let us now see what each claim amounts to.

EXTERNALIST EXPLANATIONS OF CONTENT

Since the 1970's externalism has become a widely held position in the philosophy of mind. The classic arguments for externalism are found in Hilary Putnam's (1926-2016) "The Meaning of 'Meaning'", Tyler Burge's "Individualism and the Mental", and Saul Kripke's *Naming and Necessity*. Putnam argues that "a better philosophy and a better science of language" must encompass the "social dimension of cognition" and the "contribution of the environment, other people, and the world" to semantics (Putnam 1975, 49). Burge argues against any theory about the mind in which "the mental natures of all a person's or animal's mental states (and events) are such that there is no necessary or deep individuative relation between the individual's being in states of those kinds and the nature of the individual's physical or social environment" (Burge 1986, 3-4).

The Twin Earth thought experiment of Putnam is the most famous argument in favor of externalism; it claims to show that two subjects can have identical internal psychological mental states but that the content of these states can be different due to particular variations in the environment. Putnam asks us to imagine a world (Twin-Earth) in which water is not composed of H_2O like it is on our world but is rather composed of XYZ. When a person (call him Oscar) says "water" on Earth the word refers to H_2O, but when a different person (call him Twin-Oscar) says "water" in a different place (on Twin-Earth) the word refers to XYZ. This seems intuitively clear; the word "water" refers to what the word is about in that particular environment (so when Oscar utters "water" that word is about H_2O in his environment). Putnam asks what would happen if Oscar is transported to Twin-Earth. Would the word "water" uttered by Oscar on Twin-Earth now refer to H_2O or XYZ? Notice that the thought experiment legislates that the only change that takes place when Oscar is transported from Earth to Twin-Earth is the change in his environment (i.e., all of his psychological states remain unchanged). Now, Putnam reasons that if knowing the meaning of a term is just a matter of being in a certain psychological state, then "water" on Twin-Earth when uttered by Oscar should refer to H_2O and not to XYZ as we might expect. This is because Oscar's psychological state was fixed on Earth, and if the psychological state fixes the reference then "water" refers to H_2O regardless of the environment the subject is in (Putnam 1975).

Another way to put the matter is as follows: when Twin-Oscar on Twin-Earth says "water" whilst pointing to a lake that is entirely composed of XYZ, as all watery things are composed of on Twin-Earth, "water" refers to XYZ and not to H_2O. But, Putnam's argument claims, if knowing the meaning of a term is just a matter of being in a certain psychological state then "water" uttered on Twin-Earth by Oscar transported from Earth cannot mean XYZ and must mean H_2O. Something seems to be wrong here. If two people utter the same word in the same environment we expect that word to refer to the same thing. Thus, if we want to hold on to the claim that the meaning of a term determines its reference or extension then, the argument claims, we must concede that, as Putnam famously put it, "Cut the pie any way you like, 'meanings' just ain't in the head!" (1975, 144) That is, the claim is that mind-internal properties on their own cannot fix the meanings of words or what their reference is.

Putnam's argument is directed at the meanings of words, of course, but it was soon noticed by Colin McGinn, Tyler Burge, and others that the same argument also applies to the contents of our propositional attitudes, hence to the contents of our thoughts. The main claim of externalism, then, is that even though thoughts are said to be inside a person's head, the content of these thoughts supervene[1] on external factors in the environment of the person who has them. Thus, as Ben-Menahem remarks in regard to one of Putnam's examples, "to speak of coffee tables it does not suffice for us merely to have the concept of a coffee table, but we must be in contact with *actual* coffee tables" (Ben-Menahem 2005, 10; emphasis in original).

INTERNALIST SEMANTICS

Now, it could be objected that externalism has to be right: How could content not depend on the outside world? Surely the meaning of the word "elephant" cannot be due to only mind-internal properties. The word is about elephants, it could be argued, which are in the mind-external world, not inside the mind. As we will now see, internalists argue that there are good reasons to question the externalist claim that concepts are connected to the world in the way in which externalists claim they are. In other words, internalism does not deny the link to the outside world but rather has a different explanation of how our mind generates and interprets the content of our concepts. Internalism argues that, for the purposes of scientific inquiry into language and mind, the internal properties of the human mind are the most relevant and fruitful subject matter. Thus construed, internalism is not so much a solution to the issues that externalists grapple with. Rather, as we will see below, internalism is a different research program, and so there is a difference in the sorts of questions externalism and internalism attempt to answer.

A succinct definition of internalism is provided by Wolfram Hinzen: "Internalism is an explanatory strategy that makes the internal structure and constitution of the organism a basis for the investigation of its external function and the ways in which it is embedded in an environment" (Hinzen 2006, 139). Internalism studies the internal structure and mechanisms of an organism; the external environment comes into the picture when the internal processes are ascribed content by the theorist, thus explaining how the internal mechanisms constitute a cognitive process in a particular environment. Such content ascriptions, claim internalists, vary with the theorist's interests and aims, but the content and its ascription are not an essential part of the theory itself. So, for example, the mechanism that detects vertical lines in the visual input will be in the scope of an internalist theory, but not the representational content ascribed to the output of this mechanism. The latter could be

---

1. Supervenience here refers to a certain set of properties in virtue of which some other set is made possible. If A supervenes on B then changing anything in B would also change A. So, for example, the colour blue supervenes on a certain set of physical properties such the wavelength of light. What follows is that if we change the wavelength of the light then we also change the colour. In regard to content, the externalist claim is that content supervenes on both what's in the head and on the environment. It follows, then, that if we change the relevant features in the environment then the content would also change. Internalists, of course, reject this claim.

any number of things (the vertical line could represent the edge of a building or be part of a larger representation of a human face) but its underlying mechanism remains unchanged.

In other words, as discussed by Frances Egan in work spanning the last few decades, the internalist claim is that the computational characterization of an internal mechanism abstracts away from specific content ascriptions. So one can separate the content of, say, a visual state, from the computational machinery in virtue of which that content is made possible. For example, a particular mechanism may receive as input a certain set of parameters that require computation. The theorist then examines the output of these computations. One can imagine a mechanism that is embedded in the visual system being ascribed visual contents befitting the theory of vision. However, that same mechanism can be embedded in the auditory system and thus be ascribed different (auditory) contents that are defined not in terms of visual properties but rather in terms of acoustical properties. In other words, there is nothing inherent to the internalist computations performed that makes them visual or auditory. As Egan has discussed, there is an underlying set of computations that are required for both visual and auditory processing. The label we give to the output of such computations (the content we ascribe to them) depends on where the input to the mechanism came from. If the input is visual then the theorist will ascribe the output of the mechanism a visual content. But nothing in the internal mechanism itself tells us that. Internalism studies the internal mechanism itself, which remains unchanged regardless of whether it happens to be embedded or used by, say, the visual system or the auditory system.

Let us unpack these claims. First, note that the externalist claim that states of individual organisms cannot be understood in complete isolation from the environment in which they happen to be is not in dispute. The argument is about whether what happens in the environment should be part of what the theory is supposed to explain. So what is the problem that internalists see with the externalists' relation between words and the things words are used to talk about? In a classic paper that formed one of the foundations of internalist semantics, Jerrold Katz (1932-2002) and Jerry Fodor (1935-2017) discussed this issue (though they did not frame it in terms of internalism versus externalism). Katz and Fodor ask the reader to compare the following three sentences:

(1) "Should we take junior back to the zoo?"

(2) "Should we take the lion back to the zoo?"

(3) "Should we take the bus back to the zoo?"

They then remark that information that figures in the choice of the correct interpretation for each of these sentences includes the fact that, say, lions, but not children and busses, are often kept in cages. That is, unlike (2), the meaning of (1) cannot be that we should take a living being back to the zoo and put them in a cage. (1) means that we should take a child and show them the animals around the zoo. (3), on the other hand, has neither of these interpretations. (3) cannot mean that we should take the bus to the zoo and put it in a cage, nor can it mean that we should take the bus and show it the animals around the zoo. In order to decipher these meanings one needs to know certain facts about the world; these facts are not semantic or grammatical facts (Katz and Fodor 1963).

After listing a handful of other examples of what information is needed for interpretation, Katz and

Fodor note that the reader will find it easy to construct an ambiguous sentence whose resolution requires the prior representation of practically any relevant item of information about the world. This is because, in order to resolve a great deal of ambiguous sentences, one needs to have certain facts about the world without which certain interpretations of sentences are unavailable. For example, consider the sentence "I saw the man with the binoculars." If one didn't know what binoculars were, then the only interpretation available would be that a person saw a man holding an object that is called "binoculars." However, once one's world knowledge is expanded to include facts about binoculars (namely, that they are used to see objects far away) then further interpretations become available and then the sentence becomes ambiguous. That is, the sentence then has the additional interpretation that "I saw a man and I used binoculars to see that man." Katz and Fodor's claim is that in order to disambiguate such sentences one needs to know things that are not purely semantic (what binoculars are used for is a fact about the world and not a grammatical fact). The problem is that a theory of meaning that aims to include all relevant information that is needed in order to disambiguate sentences and determine the correct interpretation will run into great difficulties, for such a theory cannot predict in advance what sort of information will be needed for sentence interpretation.

The upshot is that a theory that insists (as externalism does) on including the mind's relations to the external world in a theory of language cannot hope to find reliable relations of the sort described above (let alone systematizing them into a fruitful explanatory theory). However, in regard to the underlying mechanisms of the mind in virtue of which the generation and interpretation of content is made possible, internalists claim that a fruitful theory is possible. The most famous proponent of internalist semantics is Noam Chomsky, and his work stands in stark contrast to the externalist semantics of Hilary Putnam or Donald Davidson (1917-2003). The recent work of Paul Pietroski (2008, 2010) is an excellent example of internalist semantics. Pietroski construes meaning in terms of blueprints that are used by the language faculty in the mind in order to construct concepts. This is an attempt to explain the underlying mental mechanisms in virtue of which we can generate and interpret thought contents. The meaning of a word in internalist semantics is cashed out not in terms of the word's relation to the outside world but rather in terms of the word's internal role in the mind's construction of the concept that has the required content. Note the difference here. Internalist semantics studies the mechanisms in the mind that build concepts. Once these concepts are generated they are transferred from the language faculty to the mind-internal systems of thought and to the articulatory-perceptual system.[2] These systems then make use of concepts for various ends such as thinking and talking about the world.

In other words, the internalist claim is that the mind has certain mechanisms that include instructions to build concepts, which then provide the inputs to other (mind-internal) systems that enter into various human actions, one of which is communication. Internalist semantics, then, concerns the nature of the computational mechanisms of the language faculty and their relation to the systems of thought; it concerns not the concepts themselves but the mechanisms that fetch, build, and combine concepts within the mind. That is, internalism is concerned with the mind-internal mechanisms of concept creation. This is of course one step removed from what externalist semantics studies,

2. This is the system responsible for externalising language via sound or sign. The way a particular word is pronounced, for example, will be determined by the articulatory-perceptual system, whereas the word's meaning will be determined by the systems of thought (sometimes known as the conceptual-intentional system).

which are the concepts themselves, their role in language use, and their relation to the speaker's environment.

CONCLUSION

The difference between the externalist and internalist position in regard to mental content is a difference in the sort of questions that each attempts to answer. It is a difference in the way in which each construes the role that content plays in the explanation of language and mind. The argument in favor of either approach to the science and philosophy of language and mind is of course not a knockdown argument, nor is it a guarantee that one side will turn out to be the correct path. As Gabriel Segal correctly remarks, "The point is that we should not expect to discover too much from the armchair. Discovering the true nature of content should be a scientific enterprise (whether we also call it 'philosophical' or not)" (Segal 2000, 20).

REFERENCES

Ben-Menahem, Yemima, ed. 2005. *Hilary Putnam*. Cambridge: Cambridge University Press.

Brentano, Franz. (1874) 1995. *Psychology from an Empirical Standpoint*. London: Routledge.

Burge, Tyler. 1986. "Individualism and Psychology." *The Philosophical Review* 95(1).

Hinzen, Wolfram. 2006. "Internalism about Truth." *Mind & Society* 5.

Katz, Jerrold and Jerry A. Fodor. 1963. "The Structure of a Semantic Theory." *Language* 39(2): 170-210.

McGinn, Colin. 1989. *Mental Content*. Oxford: Blackwell.

Pietroski, Paul M. 2008. "Minimalist Meaning, Internalist Interpretation." *Biolinguistics* 2(4) (2008): 317-341.

Pietroski, Paul M. 2010. "Concepts, Meanings and Truth: First Nature, Second Nature and Hard Work." *Mind & Language* 25(3): 274-278.

Putnam, Hilary. 1975. "The Meaning of 'Meaning.'" *Minnesota Studies in the Philosophy of Science* 7.

Segal, Gabriel M. 2000. *A Slim Book about Narrow Content*. Cambridge, MA: MIT Press.

FURTHER READING

On Concepts

Baker, Mark. 2001. *The Atoms of Language: The Mind's Hidden Rules of Grammar*. New York: Basic Books.

Block, Ned. 1986. "Advertisement for a Semantics for Psychology." In Peter A. French, Theodore E. Uehling and Howard K. Wettstein, eds. *Studies in the Philosophy of Mind*. Minneapolis: University of Minnesota Press.

Carey, Susan. 2009. *The Origin of Concepts*. Oxford: Oxford University Press.

Fodor, Jerry. 1998. *Concepts: Where Cognitive Science Went Wrong.* New York: Oxford University Press.

Fodor, Jerry. 1975. *The Language of Thought.* Cambridge, MA: Harvard University Press.

Fodor, Jerry. 2008. *LOT 2: The Language of Thought Revisited.* New York: Oxford University Press.

Jackendoff, Ray. 1989. What is a Concept, that a Person may Grasp It? *Mind & Language* 4: 68-102.

McGilvray, James. 2002. "MOPs: The Science of Concepts." In Wolfram Hinzen and Hans Rott, eds. *Belief and Meaning: Essays at the Interface.* Frankfurt: Ontos.

Pinker, Steven. 2007. *The Stuff of Thought: Language as a Window into Human Nature.* London: Penguin.

On Internalism

Chomsky, Noam. 1995. "Language and Nature." *Mind* 104(416): 1-59.

Chomsky, Noam. 2000. *New Horizons in the Study of Language and Mind.* Cambridge: Cambridge University Press.

Chomsky, Noam. 2013. "What Kind of Creatures are We?" *The Journal of Philosophy* 90(12): 645-700.

Egan, Frances. 2014. "How to Think about Mental Content." *Philosophical Studies* 170: 115-135.

Farkas, Katalin. 2003. "Does Twin Earth Rest on a Mistake?" *Croatian Journal of Philosophy* 3(8): 155-69.

Lohndal, Terje and Hiroki Narita. 2009. "Internalism as Methodology." *Biolinguistics* 3(4): 321-331.

McGilvray, James. 1998. "Meanings are Syntactically Individuated and Found in the Head." *Mind & Language* 13(2): 225-280.

Mendola, Joseph. 2009. *Anti-Externalism.* Oxford: Oxford University Press.

Pietroski, Paul M. 2010. "Concepts, Meanings and Truth: First Nature, Second Nature and Hard Work." *Mind & Language* 25(3): 247-278.

Segal, Gabriel M. 2000. *A Slim Book about Narrow Content.* Cambridge, MA: MIT Press.

On Externalism

Ben-Menahem, Yemima, ed. 2005. *Hilary Putnam.* Cambridge: Cambridge University Press.

Burge, Tyler. 1979. "Individualism and the Mental." *Midwest Studies in Philosophy* 4: 73-121.

Davidson, Donald. 1987. "Knowing One's Own Mind." *Proceedings and Addresses of the American Philosophical Association* 60(3): 441-458.

Davies, Martin. 1993. "Aims and Claims of Externalist Arguments." *Philosophical Issues* 4: 227-249.

Farkas, Katalin. 2003. "What is Externalism?" *Philosophical Studies* 112(3): 187-208.

Fodor, Jerry. 1994. *The Elm and the Expert: Mentalese and its Semantics.* Cambridge, MA: MIT Press.

Horwich, Paul. 2005. *Reflections on Meaning.* Oxford: Oxford University Press.

Kripke, Saul. 1980. *Naming and Necessity.* Oxford: Blackwell.

McGinn, Colin. 1989. *Mental Content.* Oxford: Blackwell.

Millikan, Ruth. 1984. *Language, Thought and Other Biological Categories.* Cambridge, MA: MIT Press.

Nuccetelli, Susana, ed. 2003. *New Essays on Semantic Externalism and Self-Knowledge.* Cambridge, MA: MIT Press.

Pessin, Andrew and Sanford Goldberg, eds. 1996. *The Twin Earth Chronicles: Twenty Years of Reflection on Hilary Putnam's "The Meaning of 'Meaning.'"* New York: M. E. Sharpe.

Putnam, Hilary. 1975. "The Meaning of 'Meaning.'" *Minnesota Studies in the Philosophy of Science* 7: 131-193.

Wikforss, Åsa. 2008. "Semantic Externalism and Psychological Externalism." *Philosophy Compass* 3(1): 158-181.

CHAPTER 8.

FREEDOM OF THE WILL

DANIEL HAAS

INTRODUCTION: ARE WE FREE?

How much control do people exercise over who they are and what they do? Suppose it is the night before an exam, and Quinn should be studying, but her roommate asks her to come out with her and some friends. It certainly seems like it is up to Quinn what she does. She could stay home and study or she could spend the night out with friends. The choice seems hers to make and up to her. And when Quinn arrives exhausted to her exam the following morning, Quinn should feel justified blaming herself for failing to do what she should have done and what she could have done.

Or, suppose you are weighing the pros and cons between a career in something with a reasonable return on investment, like nursing or accounting, versus a career in a field with more questionable career prospects, like philosophy. Again, the choice seems yours to make. You're free to pursue whatever career path you want and it is ultimately up to you what you decide to do with your life. Right?

But maybe this sense of freedom is a mere illusion. Maybe Quinn's decision to go out with her friends the night before a big exam is an inevitable, deterministic consequence of the past and the laws of nature in such a way that her supposed freedom is undermined. Or perhaps it is the case that the real reason someone chooses a career in philosophy over a career in accounting has more to do with unconscious brain processes and the environment and social situation they find themselves in then it has to do with any conscious decision they may have made. And if so, if our choices are really the causal results of unconscious brain processes or external environmental factors, are any of us really free? Are we really in control of who we are and what we do? Or are free-will skeptics correct to claim that the things we do and the way that we are is ultimately the consequent of external factors beyond our control?

To investigate whether or not humans sometimes act freely, we need to first clarify what is meant by free will. The discussion of freedom has a long history and free will has been used to apply to a multitude of, often radically different, abilities and capacities that people may, or may not, have.

A helpful place to start is to note that most philosophers today who write on free will have in mind the kind of control required for morally responsible action (McKenna and Pereboom 2016, 6-7). That is, to ask whether or not someone is free is to ask whether or not they have control over their actions such that they are deserving of blame or praise for what they do (or fail to do).

DETERMINISM AND FREEDOM

Determinism and free will are often thought to be in deep conflict. Whether or not this is true has a lot to do with what is meant by determinism and an account of what free will requires.

First of all, determinism is not the view that free actions are impossible. Rather, determinism is the view that at any one time, only one future is physically possible. To be a little more specific, determinism is the view that a complete description of the past along with a complete account of the relevant laws of nature logically entails all future events.[1]

Indeterminism is simply the denial of determinism. If determinism is incompatible with free will, it will be because free actions are only possible in worlds in which more than one future is physically possible at any one moment in time. While it might be true that free will requires indeterminism, it's not true merely by definition. A further argument is needed and this suggests that it is at least possible that people could sometimes exercise the control necessary for morally responsible action, even if we live in a deterministic world.

It is worth saying something about fatalism before we move on. It is really easy to mistake determinism for fatalism, and fatalism does seem to be in straightforward conflict with free will. Fatalism is the view that we are powerless to do anything other than what we actually do. If fatalism is true, then nothing that we try or think or intend or believe or decide has any causal effect or relevance as to what we actually end up doing.

But note that determinism need not entail fatalism. Determinism is a claim about what is logically entailed by the rules/laws governing a world and the past of said world. It is not the claim that we lack the power to do other than what we actually were already going to do. Nor is it the view that we fail to be an important part of the causal story for why we do what we do. And this distinction may allow some room for freedom, even in deterministic worlds.

An example will be helpful here. We know that the boiling point for water is 100°C. Suppose we know in both a deterministic world and a fatalistic world that my pot of water will be boiling at 11:22am today. Determinism makes the claim that if I take a pot of water and I put it on my stove, and heat it to 100°C, it will boil. This is because the laws of nature (in this case, water that is heated to 100°C will boil) and the events of the past (I put a pot of water on a hot stove) bring about the boiling water. But fatalism makes a different claim. If my pot of water is fated to boil at 11:22am today, then no matter what I or anyone does, my pot of water will boil at exactly 11:22am today. I could try to empty the pot of water out at 11:21. I could try to take the pot as far away from a heating source as possible. Nonetheless, my pot of water will be boiling at 11:22 precisely because it was fated that this would happen. Under fatalism, the future is fixed or preordained, but this need not be the case in a

[1] I have hidden some complexity here. I have defined determinism in terms of logical entailment. Sometimes people talk about determinism as a causal relationship. For our purposes, this distinction is not relevant, and if it is easier for you to make sense of determinism by thinking of the past and the laws of nature causing all future events, that is perfectly acceptable to do.

deterministic world. Under determinism, the future is a certain way because of the past and the rules governing said world. If we know that a pot of water will boil at 11:22am in a deterministic world, it's because we know that the various causal conditions will hold in our world such that at 11:22 my pot of water will have been put on a heat source and brought to 100°C. Our deliberations, our choices, and our free actions may very well be part of the process that brings a pot of water to the boiling point in a deterministic world, whereas these are clearly irrelevant in fatalistic ones.

THREE VIEWS OF FREEDOM

Most accounts of freedom fall into one of three camps. Some people take freedom to require merely the ability to "do what you want to do." For example, if you wanted to walk across the room, right now, and you also had the ability, right now, to walk across the room, you would be free as you could do exactly what you want to do. We will call this easy freedom.

Others view freedom on the infamous "Garden of Forking Paths" model. For these people, free action requires more than merely the ability to do what you want to do. It also requires that you have the ability to do otherwise than what you actually did. So, If Anya is free when she decides to take a sip from her coffee, on this view, it must be the case that Anya could have refrained from sipping her coffee. The key to freedom, then, is alternative possibilities and we will call this the alternative possibilities view of free action.

Finally, some people envision freedom as requiring, not alternative possibilities but the right kind of relationship between the antecedent sources of our actions and the actions that we actually perform. Sometimes this view is explained by saying that the free agent is the source, perhaps even the ultimate source of her action. We will call this kind of view a source view of freedom.

Now, the key question we want to focus on is whether or not any of these three models of freedom are compatible with determinism. It could turn out that all three kinds of freedom are ruled out by determinism, so that the only way freedom is possible is if determinism is false. If you believe that determinism rules out free action, you endorse a view called incompatibilism. But it could turn out that one or all three of these models of freedom are compatible with determinism. If you believe that free action is compatible with determinism, you are a compatibilist.

Let us consider compatibilist views of freedom and two of the most formidable challenges that compatibilists face: the consequence argument and the ultimacy argument.

Begin with easy freedom. Is easy freedom compatible with determinism? A group of philosophers called classic compatibilists certainly thought so.[2] They argued that free will requires merely the ability for an agent to act without external hindrance. Suppose, right now, you want to put your textbook down and grab a cup of coffee. Even if determinism is true, you probably, right now, can do exactly that. You can put your textbook down, walk to the nearest Starbucks, and buy an overpriced cup of coffee. Nothing is stopping you from doing what you want to do. Determinism does not seem to be posing any threat to your ability to do what you want to do right now. If you want to stop reading and grab a coffee, you can. But, by contrast, if someone had chained you to the chair you are sitting in,

2. Two of the more well-known classic compatibilists include Thomas Hobbes and David Hume. See: Hobbes, Thomas, (1651) 1994, *Leviathan*, ed. Edwin Curley, Canada: Hackett Publishing Company; and Hume, David, (1739) 1978, *A Treatise of Human Nature*, Oxford: Oxford University Press.

things would be a bit different. Even if you wanted to grab a cup of coffee, you would not be able to. You would lack the ability to do so. You would not be free to do what you want to do. This has nothing to do with determinism, of course. It is not the fact that you might be living in a deterministic world that is threatening your free will. It is that an external hindrance (the chains holding you to your chair) is stopping from you doing what you want to do. So, if what we mean by freedom is easy freedom, it looks like freedom really is compatible with determinism.

Easy freedom has run into some rather compelling opposition, and most philosophers today agree that a plausible account of easy freedom is not likely. But, by far, the most compelling challenge the view faces can be seen in the consequence argument.[3] The consequence argument is as follows:

1. If determinism is true, then all human actions are consequences of past events and the laws of nature.
2. No human can do other than they actually do except by changing the laws of nature or changing the past.
3. No human can change the laws of nature or the past.

---

4. If determinism is true, no human has free will.

This is a powerful argument. It is very difficult to see where this argument goes wrong, if it goes wrong. The first premise is merely a restatement of determinism. The second premise ties the ability to do otherwise to the ability to change the past or the laws of nature, and the third premise points out the very reasonable assumption that humans are unable to modify the laws of nature or the past.

This argument effectively devastates easy freedom by proposing that we never act without external hindrances precisely because our actions are caused by past events and the laws of nature in such a way that we not able to contribute anything to the causal production of our actions. This argument also seems to pose a deeper problem for freedom in deterministic worlds. If this argument works, it establishes that, given determinism, we are powerless to do otherwise, and to the extent that freedom requires the ability to do otherwise, this argument seems to rule out free action. Note that if this argument works, it poses a challenge for both the easy and alternative possibilities view of free will.

How might someone respond to this argument? First, suppose you adopt an alternative possibilities view of freedom and believe that the ability to do otherwise is what is needed for genuine free will. What you would need to show is that alternative possibilities, properly understood, are not incompatible with determinism. Perhaps you might argue that if we understand the ability to do otherwise properly we will see that we actually do have the ability to change the laws of nature or the past.

For an earlier version of this argument see: Ginet, Carl, 1966, "Might We Have No Choice?" in *Freedom and Determinism*, ed. Keith Lehrer, 87-104, Random House.

That might sound counterintuitive. How could it possibly be the case that a mere mortal could change the laws of nature or the past? Think back to Quinn's decision to spend the night before her exam out with friends instead of studying. When she shows up to her exam exhausted, and she starts blaming herself, she might say, "Why did I go out? That was dumb! I could have stayed home and studied." And she is sort of right that she could have stayed home. She had the general ability to stay home and study. It is just that if she had stayed home and studied the past would be slightly different or the laws of nature would be slightly different. What this points to is that there might be a way of cashing out the ability to do otherwise that is compatible with determinism and does allow for an agent to kind of change the past or even the laws of nature.[4]

But suppose we grant that the consequence argument demonstrates that determinism really does rule out alternative possibilities. Does that mean we must abandon the alternative possibilities view of freedom? Well, not necessarily. You could instead argue that free will is possible, provided determinism is false.[5] That is a big if, of course, but maybe determinism will turn out to be false.

What if determinism turns out to be true? Should we give up, then, and concede that there is no free will? Well, that might be too quick. A second response to the consequence argument is available. All you need to do is deny that freedom requires the ability to do otherwise.

In 1969, Harry Frankfurt proposed an influential thought experiment that demonstrated that free will might not require alternative possibilities at all (Frankfurt [1969] 1988). If he's right about this, then the consequence argument, while compelling, does not demonstrate that no one lacks free will in deterministic worlds, because free will does not require the ability to do otherwise. It merely requires that agents be the source of their actions in the right kind of way. But we're getting ahead of ourselves. Here is a simplified paraphrase of Frankfurt's case:

> Black wants Jones to perform a certain action. Black is prepared to go to considerable lengths to get his way, but he prefers to avoid unnecessary work. So he waits until Jones is about to make up his mind what to do, and he does nothing unless it is clear to him (Black is an excellent judge of such things) that Jones is going to decide not to do what Black wants him to do. If it does become clear that Jones is going to decide to do something other than what Black wanted him to do, Black will intervene, and ensure that Jones decides to do, and does do, exactly what Black wanted him to do. Whatever Jones' initial preferences and inclinations, then, Black will have his way. As it turns out, Jones decides, on his own, to do the action that Black wanted him to perform. So, even though Black was entirely prepared to intervene, and could have intervened, to guarantee that Jones would perform the action, Black never actually has to intervene because Jones decided, for reasons of his own, to perform the exact action that Black wanted him to perform. (Frankfurt [1969] 1988, 6-7)

Now, what is going on here? Jones is overdetermined to perform a specific act. No matter what happens, no matter what Jones initially decides or wants to do, he is going to perform the action Black wants him to perform. He absolutely cannot do otherwise. But note that there seems to be a crucial difference between the case in which Jones decides on his own and for his own reasons to

4. For two notable attempts to respond to the consequence argument by claiming that humans can change the past or the laws of nature see: Fischer, John Martin, 1994, *The Metaphysics of Free Will*, Oxford: Blackwell Publishers; and Lewis, David, 1981, "Are We Free to Break the Laws?" *Theoria* 47: 113-21.

5. Many philosophers try to develop views of freedom on the assumption that determinism is incompatible with free action. The view that freedom is possible, provided determinism is false is called Libertarianism. For more on Libertarian views of freedom, see: Clarke, Randolph and Justin Capes, 2017, "Incompatibilist (Nondeterministic) Theories of Free Will," *Stanford Encyclopedia of Philosophy*, https://plato.stanford.edu/entries/incompatibilism-theories/.

perform the action Black wanted him to perform and the case in which Jones would have refrained from performing the action were it not for Black intervening to force him to perform the action. In the first case, Jones is the source of his action. It the thing he decided to do and he does it for his own reasons. But in the second case, Jones is not the source of his actions. Black is. This distinction, thought Frankfurt, should be at the heart of discussions of free will and moral responsibility. The control required for moral responsibility is not the ability to do otherwise (Frankfurt [1969] 1988, 9-10).

If alternative possibilities are not what free will requires, what kind of control is needed for free action? Here we have the third view of freedom we started with: free will as the ability to be the source of your actions in the right kind of way. Source compatibilists argue that this ability is not threatened by determinism, and building off of Frankfurt's insight, have gone on to develop nuanced, often radically divergent source accounts of freedom.[6] Should we conclude, then, that provided freedom does not require alternative possibilities that it is compatible with determinism?[7] Again, that would be too quick. Source compatibilists have reason to be particularly worried about an argument developed by Galen Strawson called the ultimacy argument (Strawson [1994] 2003, 212-228).

Rather than trying to establish that determinism rules out alternative possibilities, Strawson tried to show that determinism rules out the possibility of being the ultimate source of your actions. While this is a problem for anyone who tries to establish that free will is compatible with determinism, it is particularly worrying for source compatibilists as they've tied freedom to an agent's ability to be source of its actions. Here is the argument:

1. A person acts of her own free will only if she is the act's ultimate source.

2. If determinism is true, no one is the ultimate source of her actions.

   ---

3. Therefore, if determinism is true, no one acts of her own free will. (McKenna and Pereboom 2016, 148)[8]

For elaboration on recent compatibilist views of freedom, see McKenna, Michael and D. Justin Coates, 2015, "Compatibilism," *Stanford Encyclopedia of Philosophy*, https://plato.stanford.edu/entries/compatibilism/.

You might be unimpressed by the way source compatibilists understand the ability to be the source of your actions. For example, you might that what it means to be the source of your actions is to be the ultimate cause of your actions. Or maybe you think that to genuinely be the source of your actions you need to be the agent-cause of your actions. Those are both reasonable positions to adopt. Typically, people who understand free will as requiring either of these abilities believe that free will is incompatible with determinism. That said, there are many Libertarian views of free will that try to develop a plausible account of agent causation. These views are called Agent-Causal Libertarianism. See: Clarke, Randolph and Justin Capes, 2017, "Incompatibilist (Nondeterministic) Theories of Free Will," *Stanford Encyclopedia of Philosophy*, https://plato.stanford.edu/entries/incompatibilism-theories/.

As with most philosophical arguments, the ultimacy argument has been formulated in a number of different ways. In Galen Strawson's original paper he gives three different versions of the argument, one of which has eight premises and one that has ten premises. A full treatment of either of those versions of this argument would require more time and space than we have available here. I have chosen to use the McKenna/Pereboom formulation of the argument due its simplicity and their clear presentation of the central issues raised by the argument.

This argument requires some unpacking. First of all, Strawson argues that for any given situation, we do what we do because of the way we are ([1994] 2003, 219). When Quinn decides to go out with her friends rather than study, she does so because of the way she is. She prioritizes a night with her friends over studying, at least on that fateful night before her exam. If Quinn had stayed in and studied, it would be because she was slightly different, at least that night. She would be such that she prioritized studying for her exam over a night out. But this applies to any decision we make in our lives. We decide to do what we do because of how we already are.

But if what we do is because of the way we are, then in order to be responsible for our actions, we need to be the source of how we are, at least in the relevant mental respects (Strawson [1994] 2003, 219). There is the first premise. But here comes the rub: the way we are is a product of factors beyond our control such as the past and the laws of nature ([1994] 2003, 219; 222-223). The fact that Quinn is such that she prioritizes a night with friends over studying is due to her past and the relevant laws of nature. It is not up to her that she is the way she is. It is ultimately factors extending well beyond her, possibly all the way back to the initial conditions of the universe that account for why she is the way she is that night. And to the extent that this is compelling, the ultimate source of Quinn's decision to go out is not her. Rather, it is some condition of the universe external to her. And therefore, Quinn is not free.

Once again, this is a difficult argument to respond to. You might note that "ultimate source" is ambiguous and needing further clarification. Some compatibilists have pointed this out and argued that once we start developing careful accounts of what it means to be the source of our actions, we will see that the relevant notion of source-hood is compatible with determinism.

For example, while it may be true that no one is the ultimate cause of their actions in deterministic worlds precisely because the ultimate source of all actions will extend back to the initial conditions of the universe, we can still be a mediated source of our actions in the sense required for moral responsibility. Provided the actual source of our action involves a sophisticated enough set of capacities for it to make sense to view us as the source of our actions, we could still be the source of our actions, in the relevant sense (McKenna and Pereboom 2016, 154). After all, even if determinism is true, we still act for reasons. We still contemplate what to do and weigh reasons for and against various actions, and we still are concerned with whether or not the actions we are considering reflect our desires, our goals, our projects, and our plans. And you might think that if our actions stem from a history that includes us bringing all the features of our agency to bear upon the decision that is the proximal cause of our action, that this causal history is one in which we are the source of our actions in the way that is really relevant to identifying whether or not we are acting freely.

Others have noted that even if it is true that Quinn is not directly free in regard to the beliefs and desires that suggest she should go out with her friends rather than study (they are the product of factors beyond her control such as her upbringing, her environment, her genetics, or maybe even random luck), this need not imply that she lacks control as to whether or not she chooses to act upon them.[9] Perhaps it is the case that even though how we are may be due to factors beyond our control,

9. For two attempts to respond to the ultimacy argument in this way, see: Mele, Alfred, 1995, *Autonomous Agents*, New York: Oxford University Press; and McKenna, Michael, 2008, "Ultimacy & Sweet Jane" in Nick Trakakis and Daniel Cohen, eds, *Essays on Free Will and Moral Responsibility*, Newcastle: Cambridge Scholars Publishing: 186-208.

nonetheless, we are still the source of what we do because it is still, even under determinism, up to us as to whether we choose to exercise control over our conduct.

FREE WILL AND THE SCIENCES

Many challenges to free will come, not from philosophy, but from the sciences. There are two main scientific arguments against free will, one coming from neuroscience and one coming from the social sciences. The concern coming from research in the neurosciences is that some empirical results suggest that all our choices are the result of unconscious brain processes, and to the extent choices must be consciously made to be free choices, it seems that we never make a conscious free choice.

The classic studies motivating a picture of human action in which unconscious brain processes are doing the bulk of the causal work for action were conducted by Benjamin Libet. Libet's experiments involved subjects being asked to flex their wrists whenever they felt the urge to do so. Subjects were asked to note the location of a clock hand on a modified clock when they became aware of the urge to act. While doing this their brain activity was being scanned using EEG technology. What Libet noted is that around 550 milliseconds before a subject acted, a readiness potential (increased brain activity) would be measured by the EEG technology. But subjects were reporting awareness of an urge to flex their wrist around 200 milliseconds before they acted (Libet 1985).

This painted a strange picture of human action. If conscious intentions were the cause of our actions, you may expect to see a causal story in which the conscious awareness of an urge to flex your wrist shows up first, then a ramping up of brain activity, and finally an action. But Libet's studies showed a causal story in which an action starts with unconscious brain activity, the subject later becomes consciously aware that they are about to act, and then the action happens. The conscious awareness of action seemed to be a byproduct of the actual unconscious process that was causing the action. It was not the cause of the action itself. And this result suggests that unconscious brain processes, not conscious ones, are the real causes of our actions. To the extent that free action requires our conscious decisions to be the initiating causes of our actions, it looks like we may never act freely.

While this research is intriguing, it probably does not establish that we are not free. Alfred Mele is a philosopher who has been heavily critical of these studies. He raises three main objections to the conclusions drawn from these arguments.

First, Mele points out that self-reports are notoriously unreliable (2009, 60-64). Conscious perception takes time, and we are talking about milliseconds. The actual location of the clock hand is probably much closer to 550 milliseconds when the agent "intends" or has the "urge" to act than it is to 200 milliseconds. So, there's some concerns about experimental design here.

Second, an assumption behind these experiments is that what is going on at 550 milliseconds is that a decision is being made to flex the wrist (Mele 2014, 11). We might challenge this assumption. Libet ran some variants of his experiment in which he asked subjects to prepare to flex their wrist but to stop themselves from doing so. So, basically, subjects simply sat there in the chair and did nothing. Libet interpreted the results of these experiments as showing that we might not have a free will, but we certainly have a "free won't" because we seem capable of consciously vetoing or stopping an action, even if that action might be initiated by unconscious processes (2014, 12-13). Mele points out that what might be going on in these scenarios is that the real intention to act or not act is what happens consciously at 200 milliseconds, and if so, there is little reason to think these experiments are demonstrating that we lack free will (2014, 13).

Finally, Mele notes that while it may be the case that some of our decisions and actions look like the wrist-flicking actions Libet was studying, it is doubtful that all or even most of our decisions are like this (2014, 15). When we think about free will, we rarely think of actions like wrist-flicking. Free actions are typically much more complex and they are often the kind of thing where the decision to do something extends across time. For example, your decision about what to major in at college or even where to study was probably made over a period of months, even years. And that decision probably involved periods of both conscious and unconscious cognition. Why think that a free choice cannot involve some components that are unconscious?

A separate line of attack on free will comes from the situationist literature in the social sciences (particularly social psychology). There is a growing body of research suggesting that situational and environmental factors profoundly influence human behavior, perhaps in ways that undermine free will (Mele 2014, 72).

Many of the experiments in the situationist literature are among the most vivid and disturbing in all of social psychology. Stanley Milgram, for example, conducted a series of experiments on obedience in which ordinary people were asked to administer potentially lethal voltages of electricity to an innocent subject in order to advance scientific research, and the vast majority of people did so![10] And in Milgram's experiments, what affected whether or not subjects were willing to administer the shocks were minor, seemingly insignificant environmental factors such as whether the person running the experiment looked professional or not (Milgram 1963).

What experiments like Milgram's obedience experiments might show is that it is our situations, our environments that are the real causes of our actions, not our conscious, reflective choices. And this may pose a threat to free will. Should we take this kind of research as threatening freedom?

Many philosophers would resist concluding that free will does not exist on the basis of these kinds of experiments. Typically, not everyone who takes part in situationist studies is unable to resist the situational influences they are subject to. And it appears to be the case that when we are aware of situational influences, we are more likely to resist them. Perhaps the right way to think about this research is that there all sorts of situations that can influence us in ways that we may not consciously endorse, but that nonetheless, we are still capable of avoiding these effects when we are actively trying to do so. For example, the brain sciences have made many of us vividly aware of a whole host of cognitive biases and situational influences that humans are typically subject to and yet, when we are aware of these influences, we are less susceptible to them. The more modest conclusion to draw here is not that we lack free will, but that exercising control over our actions is much more difficult than many of us believe it to be. We are certainly influenced by the world we are a part of, but to be influenced by the world is different from being determined by it, and this may allow us to, at least sometimes, exercise some control over the actions we perform.

10. Fortunately, no real shocks were administered. The subjects merely believed they were doing so.

No one knows yet whether or not humans sometimes exercise the control over their actions required for moral responsibility. And so I leave it to you, dear reader: Are you free?

REFERENCES

Frankfurt, Harry. (1969) 1988. "Alternative Possibilities and moral responsibility." In *The Importance of What We Care About: Philosophical Essays*, 10th ed. New York: Cambridge University Press.

Libet, Benjamin. 1985. "Unconscious Cerebral Initiative and the Role of Conscious Will in Voluntary Action." *Behavioral and Brain Sciences* 8: 529-566.

McKenna, Michael and Derk Pereboom. 2016. *Free Will: A Contemporary Introduction.* New York: Routledge.

Mele, Alfred. 2014. *Free: Why Science Hasn't Disproved Free Will.* Oxford: Oxford University Press.

Mele, Alfred. 2009. *Effective Intentions: The Power of Conscious Will.* Oxford: Oxford University Press.

Milgram, Stanley. 1963. "Behavioral Study of Obedience." *The Journal of Abnormal and Social Psychology* 67: 371-378.

Strawson, Galen. (1994) 2003. "The Impossibility of Moral Responsibility." In *Free Will,* 2nd ed. Edited by Gary Watson, 212-228. Oxford: Oxford University Press.

van Inwagen, Peter. 1983. *An Essay on Free Will.* Oxford: Clarendon Press.

FURTHER READING

Deery, Oisin and Paul Russell, eds. 2013. *The Philosophy of Free Will: Essential Readings from the Contemporary Debates.* New York: Oxford University Press.

Mele, Alfred. 2006. *Free Will and Luck.* New York: Oxford University Press.

ABOUT THE CONTRIBUTORS

EDITORS

Heather Salazar (book editor) is an Associate Professor of Philosophy at Western New England University. She received her PhD at University of California, Santa Barbara. Her research focuses on the intersections of metaethics and philosophy of mind in Eastern and Western philosophy and in particular on conceptions of the self and their impact on moral obligations. Her publications include *The Philosophy of Spirituality* (Brill 2018), "Descartes' and Patanjali's Conceptions of the Self" (*Journal of Indian Philosophy and Religion* 2011) and "Kantian Business Ethics" in *Business in Ethical Focus* (Broadview 2007). She is currently under contract for a monograph which assesses and contributes to neo-Kantian ethical constructivism.

Christina Hendricks (series editor) is a Professor of Teaching in Philosophy at the University of British Columbia in Vancouver, BC, Canada, where she often teaches Introduction to Philosophy courses. She is also the and also the Academic Director of the Centre for Teaching, Learning and Technology (2018-2023). Christina has been an open education researcher and advocate for a number of years, having been a BCcampus Open Textbook Fellow, an OER Research Fellow with the Open Education Group, the Creative Commons Canada representative to the CC Global Network, and a member of the Board of Directors for the Canadian Legal Information Institute.

CHAPTER AUTHORS

Eran Asoulin received his PhD at University of New South Wales. He is currently working in Sydney, Australia in linguistics, philosophy, and cognitive science, with a focus on the study of language and mind.

Paul Richard Blum is T. J. Higgins, S.J., Chair in Philosophy at Loyola University Maryland in Baltimore. He obtained his PhD at the University of Munich in Germany and his habilitation at Free University Berlin. Most of his research deals with the history of Renaissance and early modern philosophy, including the evolution of the question of immortality into philosophy of mind. His most recent book is *Nicholas of Cusa on Peace, Religion, and Wisdom in Renaissance Context* (Roderer 2018).

Tony Cheng received his PhD at University College London. He is currently visiting Centre for the Future of Intelligence, University of Cambridge, and Institut Jean Nicod, École normale supérieure, and will be joining the Department of Philosophy, NCCU, Taipei, as an Assistant Professor. He primarily works on the nature and epistemology of content and consciousness. More specific topics include perception, the senses, attention, self-awareness, spatio-temporal representations, metacognition, cognitive development, and animal minds. For more information, please visit: tonycheng.net

Daniel Haas is currently the philosophy department head and an instructor at Red Deer College. He received his PhD in Philosophy from Florida State University. He works in moral philosophy, moral psychology and the philosophy of mind and action. His research has mainly focused on issues surrounding free will and moral responsibility.

Jason Newman has a CPhil from University of California, Santa Barbara, where he studied philosophy of mind. He is interested in all the problems arising from the nature of learning and coping with these problems. Questions around what it takes to learn a language, learn to read, learn basic math facts, or even learn basic social skills are among those that interest him most. He currently teaches at Chatham Academy at Royce, and specializes in teaching students with learning differences.

Heather Salazar (see above, under Editors)

Henry Shevlin received his PhD from the City University of New York Graduate Center. He is currently a researcher at the Leverhulme Centre for the Future of Intelligence, University of Cambridge, where he leads the *Consciousness and Intelligence* project. His primary research areas are consciousness, perception, and cognitive architecture, with a particular focus on animals and artificial systems. He also has interests in topics at the intersection of ethics and cognitive science, including the question of how philosophy and psychology can contribute to the improvement of animal welfare.

Elly Vintiadis teaches philosophy at the American College of Greece. She received her PhD in 2003 from the City University of New York Graduate Center and has also taught at the Hellenic Naval Staff and Command College and at the City College of New York. Her latest publication is a co-edited volume, *Brute Facts* (Oxford University Press 2018).

PEER REVIEWER

Adriano Palma was trained in the philosophy of language and metaphysics in Europe and in the US. He taught on four different continents and is now a senior researcher at the University of KwaZulu-Natal, in Durban, South Africa.

OTHER CONTRIBUTORS

Nate Angell (formatting contributor) is an evangelist who connects people, ideas, and technologies to make things better. He has worked across a wide variety of public and private institutions, focusing on community development, digital communications, meaningful education, open technologies, and sustainable growth.

Colleen Cressman (copy editor) is a librarian who works on open-access initiatives out of the Office for Scholarly Communication at Harvard Library. She is interested especially in doing her small part to increase the free and open availability of academic philosophy to students, scholars, and enthusiasts.

Jonathan Lashley (cover designer) worked in the visual design industry before pursuing his career in education full-time. When he isn't supporting open, online, and technology-enhanced learning at public institutions across the United States, he enjoys lending his creative skills to projects like this one.

We would also like to acknowledge **the many philosophy students, faculty and researchers** who have contributed to the project by providing comments along the way, such as discussions on the Rebus Community platform when we were originally envisioning the series and what topics should be included, as well as giving feedback on drafts of chapter outlines for books. There have been many very helpful contributions from too many people to list here, and the books would not have come together without them.

FEEDBACK AND SUGGESTIONS

If you have any feedback or suggestions for the book, please use the form below.

 An interactive or media element has been excluded from this version of the text. You can view it online here: https://press.rebus.community/intro-to-phil-of-mind/?p=155

ADOPTION FORM

If you have adopted this book or made a revised/adapted version for a course, please let us know on the adoption form for the *Introduction to Philosophy* open textbook series (embedded below).

 An interactive or media element has been excluded from this version of the text. You can view it online here: https://press.rebus.community/intro-to-phil-of-mind/?p=159

Media Attributions

- CC BY by Creative Commons

REVIEW STATEMENT

Introduction to Philosophy: Philosophy of Mind, part of the *Introduction to Philosophy* series, was produced with support from the Rebus Community, a non-profit organisation building a new, collaborative model for publishing open textbooks. Critical to the success of this approach is including mechanisms to ensure that open textbooks produced with the Community are high quality, and meet the needs of all students who will one day use them. Rebus books undergo both peer review from faculty subject matter experts and beta testing in classrooms, where student and instructor feedback is collected.

This book has been peer reviewed by a subject expert from a higher education institution. The full-text received an open review from the reviewer, based on their area of expertise. The reviewer was an academic with specialist knowledge in Philosophy of Mind.

The review was structured around considerations of the intended audience of the book, and examined the comprehensiveness, accuracy, and relevance of content, as well as longevity and cultural relevance. Further review by the series editor and the copy editor focused on clarity, consistency, organization structure flow, and grammatical errors. See the review guide for more details. Changes suggested by the reviewer were incorporated by chapter authors and the book editor.

Heather Salazar (book editor), Christina Hendricks (series editor) and authors Eran Asoulin, Paul Richard Blum, Tony Cheng, Daniel Haas, Jason Newman, Henry Shevlin, Elly Vintiadis, and the team at Rebus would like to thank the reviewer for the time, care, and commitment they contributed to the project. We recognise that peer reviewing is a generous act of service on their part. This book would not be the robust, valuable resource that it is were it not for their feedback and input.

Peer reviewer: Adriano Palma, the University of KwaZulu-Natal, Durban, South Africa.

ACCESSIBILITY ASSESSMENT

A NOTE FROM THE REBUS COMMUNITY

We are working to create a new, collaborative model for publishing open textbooks. Critical to our success in reaching this goal is to ensure that all books produced using that model meet the needs of all students who will one day use them. To us, open means inclusive, so for a book to be open, it must also be accessible.

As a result, we are working with accessibility experts and others in the OER community to develop best practices for creating accessible open textbooks, and are building those practices into the Rebus model of publishing. By doing this, we hope to ensure that all books produced using the Rebus Community are accessible by default, and require an absolute minimum of remediation or adaptation to meet any individual student's needs.

While we work on developing guidelines and implementing support for authoring accessible content, we are making a good faith effort to ensure that books produced with our support meet accessibility standards wherever possible, and to highlight areas where we know there is work to do. It is our hope that by being transparent on our current books, we can begin the process of making sure accessibility is top of mind for all authors, adopters, students and contributors of all kinds on all our open textbook projects.

Below is a short assessment of eight key areas that have been assessed during the production process. The checklist has been drawn from the BCcampus Open Education Accessibility Toolkit. While a checklist such as this is just one part of a holistic approach to accessibility, it is one way to begin our work on embedded good accessibility practices in the books we support.

Wherever possible, we have identified ways in which anyone may contribute their expertise to improve the accessibility of this text.

We also welcome any feedback from students, instructors or others who encounter the book and identify an issue that needs resolving. This book is an ongoing project and will be updated as needed. If you would like to submit a correction or suggestion, please do so using the Introduction to Philosophy series accessibility suggestions form.

ACCESSIBILITY CHECKLIST

Accessibility Checklist

Category	Item	Status
Organizing Content	Content is organized under headings and subheadings	Yes
Organizing Content	Headings and subheadings are used sequentially (e.g. Heading 1, Heading 2, etc.) as well as logically (if the title is Heading 1 then there should be no other Heading 1 styles as the title is the uppermost level)	Yes
Images	Images that convey information include Alternative Text (alt-text) descriptions of the image's content or function	Yes
Images	Graphs, charts, and maps also include contextual or supporting details in the text surrounding the image	N/A
Images	Images do not rely on colour to convey information	Yes
Images	Images that are purely decorative contain empty alternative text descriptions. (Descriptive text is unnecessary if the image doesn't convey contextual content information)	N/A
Tables	Tables include row and column headers	Yes
Tables	Tables include a title or caption	Yes
Tables	Tables do not have merged or split cells	Yes
Tables	Tables have adequate cell padding	Yes
Weblinks	The weblink is meaningful in context, and does not use generic text such as "click here" or "read more"	Yes
Weblinks	Weblinks do not open new windows or tabs	Yes
Weblinks	If weblinks must open in a new window, a textual reference is included in the link information	N/A
Embedded Multimedia	A transcript has been made available for a multimedia resource that includes audio narration or instruction	N/A
Embedded Multimedia	Captions of all speech content and relevant non-speech content are included in the multimedia resource that includes audio synchronized with a video presentation	N/A
Embedded Multimedia	Audio descriptions of contextual visuals (graphs, charts, etc.) are included in the multimedia resource	N/A
Formulas	Formulas have been created using MathML	Yes
Formulas	Formulas are images with alternative text descriptions, if MathML is not an option	N/A
Font Size	Font size is 12 point or higher for body text	Yes
Font Size	Font size is 9 point for footnotes or endnotes	Yes
Font Size	Font size can be zoomed to 200%	Yes

This page provides a record of edits and changes made to this book since its initial publication. Whenever edits or updates are made in the text, we provide a record and description of those changes here. If the change is minor, the version number increases by 0.1. If the edits involve substantial updates, the edition number increases to the next whole number.

The files posted alongside this book always reflect the most recent version. If you find an error in this book, please let us know in the Rebus Community platform. (You could instead fill out an error reporting form for the book, though we prefer the discussion platform so others can see if the error has already been reported.)

We will contact the author, make the necessary changes, and replace all file types as soon as possible. Once we receive the updated files, this Version History page will be updated to reflect the edits made.

VERSION HISTORY

Version History

Version	Date	Change	Affected Web Page
1.0	10 September 2019	original	

Printed in Great Britain
by Amazon